THE ROUGH GUIDE TO
Cello

Whether you're a beginner or a pro,
whether you are about to buy a cello or you
want to learn more about the one
you already have – this book is for you.

Hugo Pinksterboer

THE ESSENTIAL TIPBOOK

Publishing Details

This first edition published May 2002 by Rough Guides Ltd, 62–70 Shorts Gardens, London WC2H 9AH

Distributed by the Penguin Group:

Penguin Books Ltd, 80 Strand, London, WC2R 0RL

Typeset in Glasgow and Minion to an original design by The Tipbook Company bv

Printed in The Netherlands by Hentenaar Boek bv, Nieuwegein

144 pp

A catalogue record for this book is available from the British Library.

1-85828-722-7

THE ROUGH GUIDE TO
Cello

Written by

Hugo Pinksterboer

THE ESSENTIAL TIPBOOK

Rough Guide Tipbook Credits

Journalist, writer and musician **Hugo Pinksterboer** has written hundreds of articles and reviews for international music magazines. He is the author of the reference work for cymbals (*The Cymbal Book*, Hal Leonard, US) and has written and developed a wide variety of musical manuals and courses.

Illustrator, designer and musician **Gijs Bierenbroodspot** has worked as an art director in magazines and advertising. While searching in vain for information about saxophone mouthpieces he came up with the idea for this series of books on music and musical instruments. Since then, he has created the layout and the illustrations for all of the books.

Acknowledgements

Concept, design, and illustrations: Gijs Bierenbroodspot

Translation: The Tipbook Company bv

Editor: Duncan Clark

IN BRIEF

Have you just started playing? Are you thinking about buying a cello? Or do you want to find out more about the instrument you already have? If so, this book will tell you everything you need to know. You'll read about buying or renting a cello; about tailpieces, tuning pegs, bridges and fingerboards; about bows and strings; about tuning and maintenance; about the history of the cello and the family of instruments it belongs to. And much more.

Essential knowledge
Having read this book, you'll be able to get the most out of your instrument, to buy the best cello for your budget, and to easily grasp any other literature on the subject, whether in magazines, books or on the Internet.

Start at the beginning
If you have just started playing, or haven't yet begun, pay particular attention to the first four chapters. If you've been playing longer, you may want to skip ahead to Chapter 5.

Glossary
Most of the cello terms you'll come across in this book are briefly explained in the glossary at the end, which doubles as an index.

CONTENTS

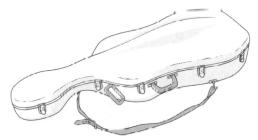

1. THE CELLO

As a cellist, you can play in all sorts of ensembles, from duos with one other person to symphony orchestras consisting of dozens of musicians. And, though most cellists stick to classical music, you can play lots of other styles too.

At first sight, cellos look a lot like violins. They're a lot bigger, though, and they sound much lower. When you play the cello, it rests between your legs, standing on a metal spike.

String instrument

The cello is a *string instrument*, just like the violin. You play both these instruments by drawing a bow across the strings, which is why they're also known as *bowed instruments*.

A beautiful sound

The cello is a very popular instrument, which isn't surprising considering what a beautiful sound it can produce. Its tone is sometimes said to resemble the human voice, and the highest-sounding string is even known as the *chanterelle*, French for 'singing string'.

A wide range

As well as a beautiful tone, the cello has a very large range, meaning it can play notes that sound both very low and extremely high. This is very useful in various different ensembles, as is the fact that the cello's tone blends well with many different instruments, from flute to piano to accordion, not to mention other string instruments and the human voice.

Different styles

Most cellists play classical music, but that doesn't mean that you can't play anything else on a cello. Cellists sometimes appear in groups playing folk, gypsy music, tango, chanson, jazz and avant-garde music, to name just a few examples. And many pop songs have a string section accompaniment.

The cello is positioned between the legs

Classical music

The cello has been around for centuries, and a great deal of music has been written for it – more than enough to keep you occupied for a lifetime. This includes music for orchestras, for smaller groups and for solo performance. Here are some examples of popular classical ensembles.

Symphony orchestras

Strings are the central feature of the biggest classical ensemble of all, the symphony orchestra, which usually has between fifty and a hundred members. In a symphony orchestra, the cellists are usually seated to the right of the conductor, as shown opposite. On the conductor's immediate right is the principal cellist, who leads the cello section; to the conductor's left is the lead violinist, also known as the *leader of the orchestra* or, in some countries, the *concertmaster*.

String sections

The cellists are one of the five groups of string instruments in an orchestra. The largest groups consist of violinists, of which there may be thirty or more, divided into *first* and *second* violinists. There are slightly fewer *violists*, who play the slightly bigger and lower-sounding viola. Then there are the cellists, and finally the *bassists*, who play the double bass, one of the lowest-sounding instruments in the orchestra.

String and cello orchestras

As well as music for symphony orchestras, there's also lots for string orchestras, which consist only of string players. And there are even orchestras made up entirely of cellists, sometimes more than fifty. These *cello orchestras* play arrangements of pieces in all sorts of styles, from classical to rock.

Other musicians

In a symphony orchestra you'll find other musicians as well, playing brass instruments (trumpet, French horn, trombone, etc), woodwind instruments (clarinet, flute, oboe, bassoon, etc) and percussion instruments (snare drums, timpani, cymbals, etc). There may also be harpists, a pianist and other instrumentalists. As shown below, the louder instruments like the trumpets and percussion instruments are toward the back, while the strings are closer to the audience.

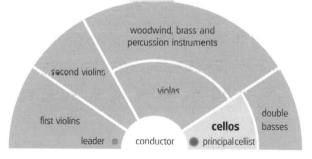

The typical arrangement of instruments in a symphony orchestra. The cellos are nearly always at the front, to the right of the conductor.

Chamber ensembles

A lot of classical music has also been written for smaller groups, collectively called chamber ensembles. Perhaps the most popular of all is the string quartet, which consists of two violinists, a violist and a cellist. There are also string quintets, which have either an extra cellist or an extra violist. Other popular chamber ensembles include the piano trio (piano, violin and cello) and the piano quartet (the same plus viola).

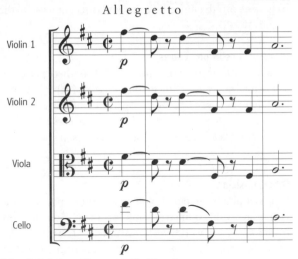

Allegretto

A few bars from a string quartet by Mozart

Duo and solo

There is also a lot of music written for duos, with the cello coupled with one other instrument. By far the most popular combination is cello and piano, but you can also play with another cellist, for example, and there is some repertoire for cello with clarinet, flute or just about any other instrument. And there are pieces that are meant to be played solo – just a cello and nothing else. This is different, of course, from the type of 'solo' playing in which you play the main part but have a whole orchestra to accompany you.

Cello or violoncello?

Most musicians call a cello a cello, but you may also come across the older name of the instrument, *violoncello*. In the past, the cello has had many other names as well – for more on the instrument's history, turn to Chapter 11, *Back in Time*.

Cello and celli

The cello is originally an Italian instrument, which explains why it's pronounced 'chello' (in Italian 'ce' is pronounced 'che'). It also explains why you may sometimes hear or read more than one cello being referred to as *celli*, which is the Italian for cellos.

2. A QUICK TOUR

A cello has a body, a neck, a fingerboard, four pegs and many other parts. This chapter tells you what everything's called and what it's for, and it also covers cellos for children.

The main part of the cello, the *body*, is the *soundbox* of the instrument: it amplifies the sound of the strings. Without the body, the instrument would hardly make any sound.

Top and back

The *top* and the *back* of the body are noticeably arched. The top, also known as the *table* or *belly*, is the most important part for the sound of the instrument. It has two *f*-shaped *soundholes* or *f-holes*.

Tuning pegs

You tune the strings using the *pegs* or *tuning pegs*. There is one for each string, at the top of the instrument, fitted in the *pegbox*.

The scroll

Right at the top is the *scroll* or *volute*. Some cellos have the head of a lion, an angel or some other shape instead of a regular scroll, though this is quite rare.

The fingerboard

The strings run along a thin, dark strip called the *fingerboard*, onto which you press your fingers to *stop* the strings. When you stop a string you make the section that is vibrating shorter, and this produces a higher note.

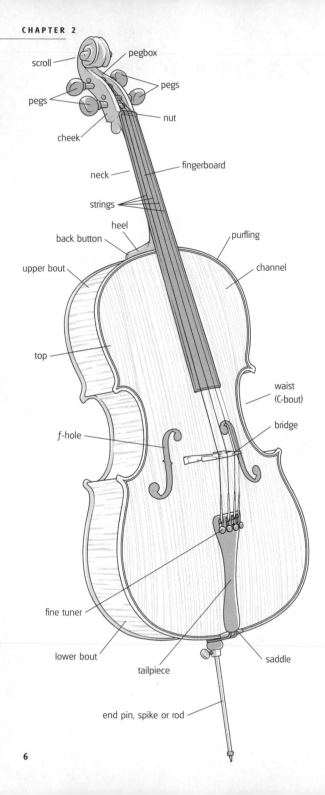

scroll

pegbox

pegs

pegs

nut

cheek

neck

fingerboard

strings

heel

back button

purfling

upper bout

channel

top

waist
(C-bout)

f-hole

bridge

fine tuner

lower bout

tailpiece

saddle

end pin, spike or rod

The neck

The fingerboard is glued onto the *neck*, which runs from the scroll to the body. However, the fingerboard is quite a bit longer than the neck, so it juts out over the body.

The nut

At the top of the fingerboard, the strings run over a small ridge called the *nut*.

The bridge

About halfway down the body, the strings run over the *bridge*, a thin piece of wood that's much lighter in colour than the rest of the cello. When you play, you make the strings vibrate with your bow. The bridge passes on those vibrations to the top, which, together with the rest of the body, amplifies the sound.

Feet

The bridge stands on the top on its two *feet*, without the help of glue or screws. The tension in the strings keeps it from falling over.

Tailpiece and fine tuners

The strings are attached to the pegs at one end and to the *tailpiece* at the other. Built-in or attached to the tailpiece there are often one or more *fine tuners*, which allow you to tune your cello more accurately and easily than with the big wooden tuning pegs.

Button, loop and saddle

The tailpiece is held in place between the strings and the *tailpiece loop*, which runs over the bottom of the cello and loops round the *end button* or *end plug*, often shortened to *button* or *plug*. To make sure this loop doesn't damage the body, the loop runs over the *saddle* or *bottom nut*.

The end pin

When you play the cello, most of the weight is taken by an adjustable metal spike – called the *end pin*, *spike* or *rod* – that protrudes from the button. The end pin can be pulled in and out to make it the right length, and when you've finished playing you can push it all the way into the instrument. To adjust the end pin, simply loosen or tighten its screw.

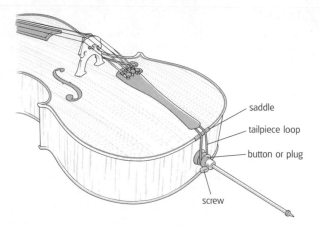

saddle
tailpiece loop
button or plug
screw

Fittings
The tailpiece, pegs and button are collectively known as the *fittings* or *trim*.

Purfling
Running along the edge of the body is inlaid *purfling*. It is usually made of three narrow strips of wood – two ebony or dark dyed strips and a lighter wood in-between.

Channel
From the edge, the top usually dips a little, before the upward arching begins. This 'valley' is called the *channel*. The back has almost the same shape.

Heel and back button
The semicircular part that sticks out at the top of the back is called the *back button*. The *heel*, the wider bottom part of the neck that links it to the body, is glued to the back button.

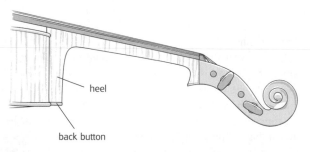

heel

back button

INSIDE

There's plenty to see inside a cello, too: the sound post, the bass bar, the maker's label and a number of small wooden blocks.

The sound post

If you look through the *f*-hole at the treble side of the instrument (by the thinnest string), you'll see a length of round wood, wedged between the top and the back. This is the *sound post*. Without one, a cello would sound very thin and hollow.

The bass bar

Near the other *f*-hole, on the bass side, is the *bass bar*. This strengthens the top and enhances the lower frequencies of the instrument. If you can take the end pin out of your cello, you'll probably be able to see both the bass bar and the sound post through the hole in the button. Some end pins are not removable.

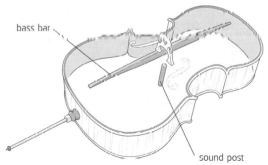

The bass bar and sound post are important to the sound of a cello

The label

If you look through the *f*-hole on the bass side, you may see the violin maker's label. Violin maker? Yes, the people who make cellos are known as violin makers. Usually, they make violins, violas and cellos, and sometimes double basses too. Violin makers are also referred to as *luthiers*.

THE BOW

To play the cello you need a bow, and the quality of the bow is as important as the quality of the instrument itself.

head

stick

bow hair

winding

bow grip

frog

screw

Bow hair and stick

The *bow hair* – usually more than two hundred hairs – almost always come from a horse's tail. One end of the hair is held in place inside the *head* or *tip*, at the top end of the *stick* or *bowstick*, and the other end is held in place inside the *frog*.

Tension

Before you play, you have to create tension in the hair by turning the *screw* clockwise. After you have played, turn the screw button anticlockwise until the hair goes slack – if you don't, the stick's elasticity will gradually decrease.

Bow grip

You hold the bow at the *grip* (or *bow grip*), which is often made of leather, and the *winding*, usually very thin metal wire. Apart from improving your bow hold, this also protects the wood.

Rosin

For the bow to do its job properly, you need to rub the hair with a piece of *rosin*. This makes the hair slightly sticky – without it, sliding the bow across the strings will hardly produce a sound.

STRINGS AND CLEFS

A cello has four strings. If you take a closer look, you can see that the strings are usually wound with ultra-thin metal ribbon. Inside this ribbon is the *core*. Most cellists use strings with a steel core, but others prefer a synthetic or gut core.

The notes

The cello strings are tuned to the notes C, G, D and A, as shown on the piano keyboard opposite. The C is the thickest and lowest-sounding string; the A is the thinnest and highest-sounding.

Very low, very high
If you go from the lowest to the very highest note you can play on a cello, you will span more than five octaves (an octave is the 'musical gap' of eight white keys on a piano). This is a bigger range than most other instruments.

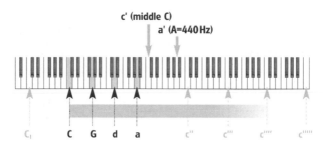

The cello's strings and range

Naming notes
In the above diagram, the note names are written in various different ways – C, a, c''' and so on. This is a system of writing down notes that allows you to refer to a specific octave (you can read more about this and other systems in *The Rough Guide to Reading Music and Basic Theory*). As you can see, the cello's A-string sounds the pitch a, the A to the left of middle C. This is one octave lower than a', the pitch which is often used for tuning instruments.

Clefs
If you take another look at the music on page 4, you'll see that the staves (the sets of five horizontal lines) are marked with a different symbol for each different instrument. This symbol is called a *clef*. The music for the violins is written using the *treble clef* or *G clef*. The music for the cello has a *bass clef* or *F clef*, and the viola uses the *alto clef*. With each clef, the lines of the staff indicate different notes.

Three clefs
Because the cello has such a big range, music for it often makes use of more than just the bass clef. The highest notes are written using the treble clef – just like the violin

– and for in-between notes there's the *tenor clef* (a C clef with middle C on the fourth line up). As a cellist, you will eventually have to learn to read music in all three of these clefs.

CHILDREN'S INSTRUMENTS

A full-size cello is too big for most children under the age of around thirteen, so smaller cellos are also available, and they come in *fractional sizes.*

Full-size cellos

A full-size cello is usually referred to as a *full-size* or *4/4 cello.* As the illustration shows, the fractions don't really describe the size of the instrument – a 1/2 cello is not really half as big as a 4/4. Besides the ones shown here, there are other fractional sizes as well.

The correct size

There are no rules about which size should go with which

The most popular cello sizes and their average string lengths

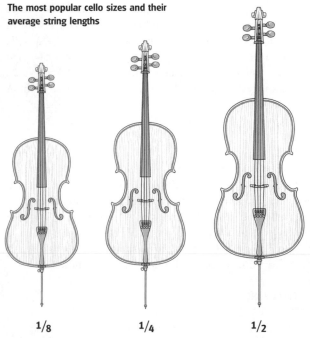

1/8	1/4	1/2
(19.29"/490mm)	(21.06"/535mm)	(23.62"/600mm)

age. One six-year-old might be better off with a 1/4 cello and another with a 1/2. And the same goes for bows. Not only do the child's finger and arm lengths count, but also factors like the strength of their fingers. Also, the sizes of the instruments vary slightly – one 1/2 cello may be a little bigger or smaller than another. So a child should always be 'fitted' with a cello by someone who knows what they're doing, such as a teacher or a knowledgeable dealer.

Smaller

Smaller cellos have a 'smaller' tone, so you shouldn't really play an instrument that is too small for you. Having said that, if you absolutely love the sound of your 7/8 cello, you may prefer it to a full-size instrument – until you find one you like even more, at least.

| 3/4 | 7/8 | 4/4 |
| (25.00"/635mm) | (26.34"/670mm) | (27.36"/695mm) |

3. LEARNING TO PLAY

The cello may not be the easiest instrument to start with, but it won't take years before you can perform on it. This chapter provides information about learning the cello: lessons, practising and ways to make it more fun.

Anyone can play any note on a piano. Just hit the right key and it sounds. On a cello it's much harder, and it takes quite a while to learn how to produce a nice and even tone by drawing the bow over the strings.

Pizzicato

You can also play the cello by plucking the strings with your fingers, which is known as *pizzicato*. Some teachers start their students off with this technique, so they can concentrate on left-hand technique before worrying about using the bow.

In tune

To play the cello in tune, you have to put your left-hand fingers in exactly the right places on the finger-board. This also takes time to learn.

Cellists have to stop the strings in exactly the right places

Stickers

Teachers have developed various techniques to make learning the cello less hard than it may sound here. One popular method is to put small stickers on the fingerboard to mark where the strings should be stopped.

LESSONS

With a good cello teacher, you'll learn about everything connected with playing the instrument – from bowing technique and reading music to sitting with good posture.

Finding a teacher

Children can sometimes have lessons in school, but adults have to find their own teachers. Music stores often have lists of private teachers, or you could ask a music teacher at a school or music college in your area for a recommen dation. Alternatively, visit your local library and ask for the ISM register of professional private music teachers or the list provided by the European String Teachers Association (see page 125 for the Web addresses of these organisations). You could also check the classified ads in newspapers, music magazines or the Yellow Pages. For individual lessons from a private teacher, expect to pay roughly £15–30 per hour.

Group lessons

Instead of taking individual lessons, you could choose to take group lessons if it's an option in your area. Lessons in schools and adult education classes are often taught like this, with one teacher to two or more pupils. They can't be tailored exactly to your needs like individual lessons, but they usually work out cheaper. Also, some teachers think that certain things are better learned in groups, so they en- courage their pupils to take both individual and group lessons.

Collectives

If you want more than just lessons you should see whether there are any music centres or colleges, or adult education centres, in your vicinity. These may offer ensembles, orchestras, master classes and more, as well as individual and group lessons.

Questions, questions

On your first visit to a teacher, don't simply ask how much it costs. Here are some other questions.

- Is an **introductory lesson** included? This is a good way to find out how well you get on with the teacher, and, for that matter, with the instrument.
- Is the teacher interested in taking you on as a student if you are just doing it **for the fun of it**, or are you expected to practise hours every day?
- Do you have to make a large investment in books and music right away, or is **course material provided**?
- Can you **record your lessons**, so that you can listen at home to how you sound, and hear once more what's been said?
- Is this teacher going to make you practise scales for years, or will the lessons be more focused on **performing pieces**?

PRACTICE

How much should you practise? That depends on what you want to achieve. Half an hour each day usually results in steady progress, but some players put in much more time than that. Either way, it's better to practise a bit every day than half a day once a week.

Keeping quiet

Cellos don't make a lot of noise, but they are loud enough to bother other people in your house when you're practising. There are various ways to overcome this. First, you can buy a *practice mute*, a short, fat comb-shaped device which

A practice mute

can be slid onto the bridge to mute much of the sound. Available in wood, metal and rubber for around £5–15, practice mutes are very useful, though they do change your sound, so it's best not to use one when you're working on your tone. Other types of mutes are discussed in Chapter 8.

Electric cello

If you want to produce even less sound, you could consider investing in an electric cello. Some of these instruments have been specifically designed for quiet practising. They make very little audible noise but have a built-in amplifier, allowing you to use headphones to hear what you're playing. Some also have special inputs for hooking up other devices such as CD players, so you can play along with pre-recorded music. There's more on electric cellos in Chapter 12, *The Family*.

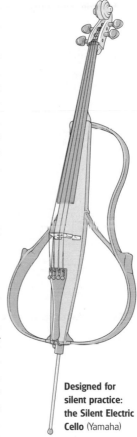

Designed for silent practice: the Silent Electric Cello (Yamaha)

On CD

Most cello music is played with other instruments, such as a piano, other strings or a complete orchestra. One way to get hold of these musicians is to buy them on CD. You can get special discs, for example, designed to help you practise cello concertos (works for orchestra and cello). They often contain the same piece recorded more than once. You may get one recording of the work complete with a cellist so you can hear how it should be done; another recorded slowly and just with piano accompaniment for while you're learning the piece; and one at full speed with a full orchestra and no cellist, leaving you to fill in the solo part. Such CDs usually come with sheet music – your local music store should be able to order them for you.

On computer

There are also CD-ROMs available that you can play along to. They are usually quite similar to the CDs described on the previous page, but they often have special features such as a tool to adjust the speed of the piece.

Metronome

Most pieces of music are supposed to be played in the same tempo from beginning to end. A good way to learn how to keep to a constant tempo is to practise with a metronome. These small mechanical or electronic devices tick or bleep a steady adjustable pulse, so you can tell immediately if you're slowing down or speeding up.

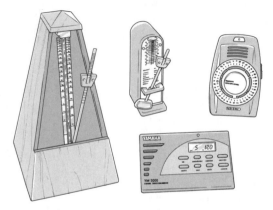

Two mechanical and two electronic metronomes

Recording

If you record your lessons, when you get home you can listen to what was said and played. This can be very helpful, and so can recording yourself playing a piece when you're practising at home – you may be surprised at how different you sound when played back. All you need is a cassette recorder with a built-in microphone, though obviously better equipment will give you better results.

Listen and play

The best way to get inspired as a cello player is listen to lots of cello music, both live and recorded. Go and watch and listen to orchestras, string quartets and other groups – living legends or local amateurs, every concert's a learning experience. But the best way to learn to play? Play a lot.

4. BUYING AND RENTING?

Cellos aren't cheap instruments – prices start at a few hundred pounds and go up to a few million. So it's definitely worth considering renting a cello when you first start playing. This chapter gives you an idea how much you should expect to spend on an instrument, whether buying or renting.

Children under twelve often start off on a rented cello, so they can easily exchange it for a larger size after they've grown a bit. Even if you are well beyond that age, renting a cello can be a good way to start, either to find out if you like playing the instrument at all or to find out if you like a specific instrument.

Rental fees
You can rent a full-sized student cello from around £30 a month, complete with bow and case, and some companies offer better rates if you agree to rent for an longer period, such as an academic year. Fractional-sized instruments are sometimes cheaper, but not always, and insurance may or may not be included. If it's not, rates for a student instrument are usually less than £10 per month. Some shops also ask for a deposit or a credit card number.

Rent-to-own
Some companies offer a rent-to-own option, meaning that if you've been renting an instrument you can choose to buy it later on, and some or all of the money you've spent on rental fees will be deducted from the price. There's a wide variety of different rental and rent-to-own deals, so

always read your agreement carefully before signing, and compare what various dealers or music shops are offering.

More expensive cellos

It's also possible to rent a more expensive instrument, so you can take your time to assess its quality. To give you a rough idea, you may rent a £30,000 instrument for around £450 per month, the rental fee equalling 1.5% of the list price.

BUYING A CELLO

If you're looking for a decent, good-sounding cello that you'll be able to enjoy playing for many years, dealers and teachers will probably advise you to spend around £1000–1500, plus at least another £250 for a basic bow and a case.

Cheaper instruments

There are, of course, plenty of people who have had years of fun playing a much less expensive instrument. After all, you can buy a complete *outfit* (cello, bow and case) for as little as £300, or even less. That said, there are cheap cellos that are barely playable unless you have a lot of work done on them – even if they are labelled 'manufacturer-adjusted'.

Shop adjustment

Basically, every mass-produced cello needs an additional adjustment in the shop before it can be played. This adjustment, also known as 'setting up' the instrument, includes making sure that the bridge, nut, sound post, fingerboard and tuning pegs perfectly fit the instrument.

Better, finer, richer

If you buy a more expensive cello, the higher price probably means that more time and attention will have been devoted to its manufacture, that better wood will have been used and that all the components will be better matched to each other. The result will be a better-looking, richer-sounding instrument, which may well also be easier to play.

Better but cheaper

That said, you may very well find a new £1000 instrument that performs and looks better than a new one priced at £1500, depending, for one thing, on where the instrument was made.

A good sound for less

The most important tip when you go to buy your first instrument is to take someone along with you who knows cellos well. They will be able to tell you if an instrument sounds much better than its price suggests, or the other way around. If you don't know any experienced cellists, try asking your teacher. And if you can't find anyone at all, at least buy from a shop where a salesperson plays the instrument.

STUDENT AND MASTER CELLOS

All kinds of names are used to classify cellos. Here's a quick run-through of what the terms mean.

Names

Sometimes you find cellos classified as student, orchestra and concert instruments. These names seem to suggest that you should start off with the first, buy an orchestra cello once you are good enough to play in an orchestra and move on to a concert cello as soon as you're ready to play a solo concert. Similarly, there are conservatory and artist cellos.

But ...

The problem with these names is that everyone has their own ideas about what they mean. For instance, some master violin makers build 'student cellos' that sell for ten times the price of a mass-produced 'concert cello'. So don't pay too much attention to the names. The price will usually tell you more.

Handmade

'Handmade' is another word that can be misleading. Plenty of low-cost production cellos have largely or entirely been built by hand – but that doesn't necessarily mean they're good instruments.

Master cellos

The term 'master cello' can be just as vague. Officially, though, master cellos are made from start to finish by a master violin maker. They usually cost around £7500 or more, and you have to be prepared to join a long waiting list for delivery. It goes without saying that a master violin maker or *luthier* does everything by hand – so there's no need to use the word 'handmade'.

Workshop cellos

The term 'workshop cello' usually refers to instruments that others may call 'intermediate' or 'step-up' cellos, in the price range of about £1000 and more. These are often good, handmade instruments, but they're produced in series, rather than by one master luthier.

Old production instruments

Older factory-made cellos can fetch a relatively high price, because many cellists believe that old instruments sound better. Even so, a brand-new cello costing £1000 may well be a better instrument than a £1500 instrument built in the early 1900s, for example.

Small cellos

Fractional-sized cellos are not always that much cheaper than full-sized instruments of the same quality, mainly because fewer of them are made. The same goes for small-sized bows, strings and cases.

BUYING TIPS

The next chapter goes into detail about exactly what to look for when testing and comparing cellos. This section provides some more general tips – things you should know before you head out to the shops. For one thing, it's always worth seeking out a shop or salesperson who knows about cellos.

Where to buy?

You can buy cellos in general music shops, though these often only sell lower-priced production instruments, or at specialized violin dealers, and at violin makers. Besides expensive handmade master cellos, many violin makers also supply more affordable instruments.

On approval

Sometimes – though usually only with expensive cellos – you may be able to take an instrument on approval, so that you can assess it at home in your own time.

Label

You can buy good cellos through classified ads in papers or at auctions, if you know what to look for, though you should always be a little cautious. There are thousands of cellos around, for example, with labels bearing the names of famous violin makers like Stradivarius. But that doesn't mean they're genuine – making labels isn't very difficult compared to making cellos.

Antonio Stradivarius Cremonenfis Faciebat Anno 1???

Anyone can make a label

Appraisals

If you find a secondhand instrument anywhere else than at a reputable violin dealer or maker, it's best to have it appraised before you buy it. Violin makers can tell you what a cello is worth, whether there's anything wrong with it and, if there is, what it will cost to put it right. An appraisal may cost about one or more percent of the value of the cello, though if that isn't much you may have to pay a minimum charge instead.

Buying online

You can also buy musical instruments online or by mail order, but this makes it impossible to compare them. Many online and mail-order companies offer some kind of return service, but even then you'll pay lots in delivery, and if there are any scratches on the instrument they may refuse to take it back. All in all, it's not a sensible option.

Take your time

It's worth taking your time when you go to buy a cello. After all, it's a serious investment, and you want it to serve you well for many years.

Fairs and conventions

One last tip: if a musical-instrument trade fair is being held in your vicinity, go along. Besides lots of instruments that can be tried out, you'll come across plenty of product specialists and numerous fellow cellists, who are always a good source of information and inspiration.

EXPENSIVE CELLOS

Professional cellists and conservatory students often play instruments worth tens of thousands of pounds, and there are even cellos that cost millions. Why are they so expensive?

Famous makers

Cellos by famous violin makers of the past like Stradivarius, Amati or Guarnerius don't cost a million pounds or more only because they're so good, but also because they're three hundred or so years old and very rare.

Better?

Age doesn't necessarily make cellos better, but it does make them more expensive. You can easily pay ten times more for an old instrument than for an equally good new one. There have been numerous blindfold tests done, in which professional violinists and cellists have failed to tell the difference between a famous old instrument and something newer, but this doesn't detract from the price of instruments by the old masters.

Less famous, less expensive

Old cellos by less famous makers are usually not as expensive as those by the big names. You may be able to buy a very good, rare German cello, for example, the same age as a Stradivarius, for less than £15,000.

Different opinions

When discussing cellos, its worth bearing in mind that opinions vary about pretty much everything – and this is as true of experts as it is of anyone else. They have different views not only about technical details, but also about general points such as what constitutes a 'decent' or a 'good' cello.

A few years or fifteen minutes

Experts also disagree about how long it takes for a new cello to start sounding really good. Some say it takes years, while others claim it takes fifteen minutes at most. Similarly, some people believe in the use of special vibrating devices that 'play in' your cello for you, and others don't.

Conservatory cellos

Some conservatory cello students are in a position to buy a good-quality instrument, but some rent an expensive cello. Others complete their education with a middle-range instrument worth a couple of thousand pounds, and some are lucky enough to be loaned an extremely valuable cello by the conservatory or some other organization.

5. A GOOD CELLO

When you first start playing, all cellos seem pretty similar, but actually there are huge differences, both in terms of sound and technical details such as varnishes, woods, tops, backs, bridges and pegs. This chapter tells you how to spot the differences when you're testing and comparing instruments, to help you pick the best possible cello for your budget.

How a cello sounds depends a lot on how it was built and on the quality of the wood. But the strings are important too, and so are the bow and the way the instrument is adjusted. These three subjects are dealt with in Chapters 6, 7 and 10 respectively.

By ear

The first and major part of this chapter is about everything there is to see on a cello, and what it all means for how the instrument sounds. If you'd prefer to choose a cello using your ears only, then turn to the tips on pages 45–47.

THE LOOKS

Cellos come with glossy and mat finishes, and some have a warm, satin-like glaze. When it comes to colour there are even more variations. Some are pale orange or even yellowish, some have a rich amber or deep-brown hue, and others tend towards red or purple. Cellos in completely different colours, such as green or blue, are very rare – but they do exist.

Oil and spirit

Traditionally, cellos have an oil-based finish, which used to take weeks to dry. Today, these finishes can be dried using ultraviolet light, and you may be able to find oil-varnished cellos for as little as £600. Spirit-based varnishes are used on cellos in most price ranges, often hand-rubbed rather than sprayed or brushed.

Invisible repairs

No one finish is typically better than any other: if you have to choose between two cellos with different finishes, don't go for the finish but for the instrument as a whole. What's important is that repairs and scratches can be touched up invisibly with both oil-based and spirit based varnishes.

Synthetic varnishes

Low-priced cellos sometimes have a synthetic finish such as polyurethane. These glossy finishes can be applied very quickly, using spray guns, and they're strong, hard and easy to clean. Being so hard, on the other hand, they may reduce the instrument's sound potential, especially when applied in thick layers. Another drawback is that they don't allow for invisible repairs.

Shading

Cellos are not always the same colour all over. Older instruments sometimes have a lighter patch where the left hand touches the body, for instance. These worn-out patches are sometimes imitated on new cellos, too, to make them look older than they are. This technique is called *shading*.

Craquelure

On older cellos, the varnish is sometimes marked with *craquelure*, thousands of tiny cracks like you see on some old paintings. But this effect, too, can be imitated by modern cello makers. Yet another way to make an instrument look older is to apply a dark dye to bring out the grain.

Aged to order

Antiquing is a general name for making a cello look older than it is, which often raises its price. If you have an instrument custom-built, you can of course ask to have it 'antiqued'. Even minor damage and worn-out spots can be imitated.

Flamed wood

A bookmatched flamed back

The wood of the backs and ribs of many cellos looks like it's been licked by flames. This *flamed, figured* or *curled wood* is commonly used for more expensive instruments, but you may also find it in the lower price ranges. Whether the wood is plain, slightly flamed or extremely flamed does not affect its quality or sound potential. But beautifully flamed wood does have its price: in student and intermediate price ranges, the heavily flamed instruments are often the more expensive ones.

Bookmatched

Many flamed backs are clearly made up of two precisely mirrored or *bookmatched* halves (see pages 110–111).

The scroll

Something else to look at is the scroll. They vary in terms of the number of windings (most have three), the degree to which the centres (the *ears*) stick out, and the type of *fluting* (the carved grooves in the back). The scroll is sometimes referred to as the *signature* of the instrument, and experts can tell the maker of a cello by examining the scroll.

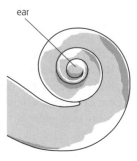

ear

The scroll: the maker's signature

Purfling

The inlaid purfling is not just for decoration. It also prevents cracks at the edge of the cello from extending to the *plates* (top and back). Double purfling, a characteristic of the Brescian school (see page 117), is rare, but you may come across it. A tip: on very inexpensive cellos, the purfling is sometimes not inlaid, but painted, or scratched into the wood and dyed.

single purfling   double purfling

Purfling usually consists of three or more inlaid strips of wood

THE BODY

Some instruments may have noticeably wider bodies than
others, or just a wider or a slimmer waist (the *C-bout*), and
some cellos are slightly shorter or taller. Generally speaking,
a larger body will give you a slightly larger sound.

The ribs

Cellos vary in their depth, too. A relatively shallow instrument – one with low *ribs* – may sound quite thin, and a
cello that is too deep may have a hollow sound. A cello is
always a little deeper at the tail than it is at the top of the
body.

String length

The standard *string length*, the distance from the nut to the
bridge, is 27.36" (695mm), but it does vary between
instruments. If you're testing a cello and find yourself
playing out of tune more than usual, it could be due to a
different string length or because of a different *mensur ratio*
(for more on this, turn to the glossary entry for string length
on page 122). This can be off-putting at first, but generally
it doesn't take too long to get used to an instrument with
slightly different dimensions.

The top

The top is the single most important part of a cello. When
you play, the strings make the top vibrate, and it is mainly
these vibrations that determine the sound of the instrument. This explains why the top is often referred to as the
soundboard.

Spruce

The top is almost always made of solid spruce. Spruce is also used for the bass bar and the sound post.

Maple

The back is usually made of one or two carved pieces of solid maple, a heavier and denser wood that is also used for the ribs and the neck. However, one-piece backs are often made of other types of wood, such as willow or poplar, both of which are softer and result in a slightly softer, warmer sound.

Laminated wood

Cheaper cellos may have a laminated back or top made up of several plies (layers) of wood. These plywood plates are very durable and crack-resistant, but they do not make for a rich, musical sound. If you're not sure whether the plates are solid or laminated, check the edges of the *f*-holes.

Fine grain

Cellists often prefer the top to have a grain that is straight, even and not too wide, getting gradually finer toward the centre of the instrument. There are no hard-and-fast rules, though, about what's best. Some cellos have a beautiful grain but don't sound very good, and there are great instruments with a wide, uneven or wavy grain.

The arching

A top with a lower arching will usually help produce a stronger, more powerful and direct sound; a higher arching may contribute to a softer, warmer timbre. Most modern cello tops are slightly over an inch (around 2.5cm) high. The back is usually a little flatter.

The back is a little flatter than the top

The channel

A cello with a deep, broad channel will often have a softer

sound than an instrument that barely has this 'valley' along the edge.

Flowing lines

You can spend hours looking at the arching of cello tops. They all look quite similar at first, but each is slightly different – the more often you look, the more obvious the differences will be. It's important that the lines of the arch flow, that there are no flat parts or odd angles, and that the arching isn't too high, too low or too narrow.

Thick and thin

Low-cost cellos often have quite thick tops or backs, which are easier to make. If they're too thick, the instrument may sound quite thin. Good instruments have *graduated* plates, their exact thickness varying from spot to spot. The top usually varies from about 0.19" (4.75mm) in the middle to 0.14" (3.6mm) at the edges. The back is a little thicker overall.

Hot hide glue

Most good-quality cellos are assembled using animal glue (*hot hide glue*). Joints fixed with this type of glue can be loosened, which means that the top can be taken off, for example, to allow repairs inside the instrument. Also, this type of glue will 'let go' if the wood shrinks or expands as a result of age or changes in humidity. This prevents the plates from cracking; all the violin maker has to do is to apply new glue. And the overhang of the edges means that such repairs can be made invisible.

NECK AND FINGERBOARD

The neck and fingerboard affect not only the playability, but also the sound of a cello.

Ebony

The smoother and more even the fingerboard, the more easily the instrument will play. Most fingerboards are made of ebony, an extremely dark and hard wood. Cheap cellos sometimes have fingerboards made of softer, lighter-coloured wood, often painted black to make it look like ebony. You can sometimes recognize such fingerboards by lighter patches or spots on the sides. Bear in mind, though, that the use of ebony is not a guarantee for a good fingerboard: cheaper, softer types of ebony do exist.

Wear
After years of use, even the hardest fingerboard will wear down. When this starts happening, it should be reworked and, eventually, replaced (see Chapter 10, *Cello Maintenance*).

Clearance
The fingerboard has a curved top, similar to the top of the bridge. On most fingerboards, though, the area under the C-string has been flattened. This provides extra clearance for the wide vibrations of this string, preventing it from rattling against the fingerboard. These fingerboards, introduced by the German cellist Bernard Romberg in the mid-nineteenth century, are recognizable by the 'ridge' between the G- and the C-string.

Thick fingers
The grooves in the nut, at the top of the fingerboard, determine the string spacing and the string height at that end. Nuts can be replaced to adjust both these factors. For example, if you have thick fingers, you may prefer a nut with grooves set quite far apart.

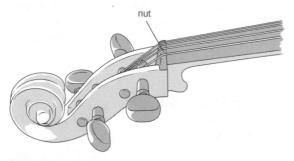

nut

The nut can be replaced

Feel the neck
Necks are always much lighter in colour that the body – a dark neck would soon show up worn patches. On more expensive cellos, the wood is usually not varnished but protected with an oil finish. When testing a cello, feel

whether the curve of the neck lies nicely in your hand, and make sure there are no odd pits or bumps on it.

Concave fingerboard

The fingerboard is very slightly concave if you look from the side. If it isn't, the strings may rattle against the fingerboard in certain positions.

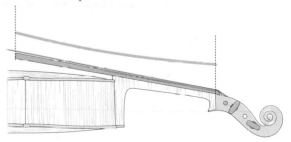

Fingerboards are slightly concave

Straight

If you look at the neck and fingerboard lengthways, they should be straight and set exactly in the centre of the cello. Take a good look along the fingerboard from the scroll towards the bridge. Also check whether the strings run perfectly straight along the fingerboard (though remember that this requires a properly installed tailpiece and bridge).

Backwards

The neck of a modern cello is tilted backwards slightly. Before the 1800s, there was a ninety-degree angle between the neck and the body. These instruments sounded softer, as the larger neck angle reduced the pressure of the strings on the bridge. Conversely, a smaller neck angle means more pressure on the bridge, which makes the sound bigger, louder and more radiant.

neck angle

A smaller neck angle gives a bigger sound

Baroque cello

The larger neck angle is one of the characteristics of the Baroque cello, which some cellists still use today to play music of the Baroque era (c.1600–1750). Its mellow, gentle sound is the partly the result of its neck angle, though a lower bridge, a shorter neck, a different bow, gut strings and lower tuning are also factors.

STRING HEIGHT

The string height is the distance between the strings and the fingerboard. If the strings are very high above the fingerboard, the cello will be hard work to play. If they are too low, they may rattle. In-between, it's largely a matter of taste and the type of strings you're using. A greater string height can give your instrument a slightly clearer, brighter or more powerful sound.

Room to move

At the nut, the gap between the strings and the fingerboard is very small. At the other end of the fingerboard it's a lot bigger, especially above the thick strings, which are given extra height because they need more room to vibrate.

The figures

As a rule of thumb, if you use steel-core strings, the A-string should be about 0.18–0.22" (4.5–5.5mm) above the end of the fingerboard, and the C-string about 0.26–0.30" (6.5–7.5mm). Gut strings are usually set about 0.04" (1mm) higher, and synthetic-core strings are somewhere in-between the two.

Too high

If you have a new cello that has not yet been properly adjusted, the strings will probably be too high. The adjustment process may involve having the bridge and the nut adapted.

THE BRIDGE

The bridge matters not only for the string height, but also for the sound of a cello.

Between the notches

Bridges are a bit slanted at the front and straight at the back. The straight back should be perpendicular to the instrument's top, and the middle of the bridge's feet should be exactly between the notches of the *f*-holes – though some instruments sound better if the bridge is moved forward or backward a tiny bit.

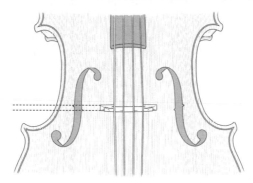

The bridge is positioned between the notches of the *f*-holes

Flecked

Some bridges are plain while others are flecked. In itself, this difference tells you nothing about the quality of the wood: plain, slightly flecked and highly flecked woods are all used for both cheap and expensive bridges. A fine, straight grain is more impor-tant.

Flecked wood tells you nothing about the quality of a bridge

Treated and untreated

String-instrument catalogues often indicate whether bridges are treated or untreated, which refers to whether or not they are finished with varnish or oil.

Too heavy, too light

Obviously, you're not going to weigh the bridge when you're choosing a cello, but it's worth knowing that a heavy bridge can muffle the sound slightly, just like a mute (see pages 71–74). A very light bridge may be the culprit if an instrument has a very thin, weak or uncentred tone. The hardness of the wood also plays a role. A bridge made of harder wood ensures more volume and a stronger, brighter tone.

French and Belgian bridges

Cello bridges come in two basic models. The *French bridge* has shorter legs and longer wings, while *Belgian bridges* have longer legs and less mass. Soundwise, a French bridge enhances the lower frequencies of an instrument and makes the sound a bit mellower. Belgian bridges help create a brighter, more pronounced sound and a lot of clarity on the D- and A-strings.

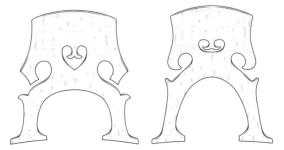

A French bridge (left) and a Belgian bridge (right)

Blanks

The bridges you find in stores and catalogues are *blanks*: bridges always need to be custom-fitted to your instrument. There are bridges with moveable feet that automatically adjust to the arch of the top, but even if you prefer this type the bridge should be installed by a professional: fitting a bridge properly involves more than carving the feet (see pages 94–95).

Too deep

Bridges don't last forever. Eventually, the strings wear into the wood and the grooves become too deep, resulting in muffled strings and harder tuning. The string height will be decreased as well, and the strings may break sooner. Ideally, the grooves should be just deep enough so that two-thirds of the thickness of each string sticks out above the bridge.

The A-string

The A is the string that is most likely to cut into your bridge. This can be prevented by putting a plastic sleeve (see page 55) or a piece of vellum (parchment) under the string. Some bridges have a bone or hardwood insert for the same purpose.

A bridge with an ebony inset

Two at once

The top of the bridge has almost the same curve as the top of the fingerboard: it is highest in the middle and lowest by the thinnest string. Beginner cellists often prefer a highly curved bridge, as this reduces the chance of inadvertently bowing two strings instead of one.

Collapsed bridges

Nearly all bridges collapse slightly over time, due to the pressure of the strings. A cello will only produce its best sound with a straight bridge, so it's worth checking yours from time to time (see pages 93–94).

Height and tone

The bridge height influences both string height and tone. A slightly higher bridge increases the string tension, which makes the sound a little brighter or stronger. If the bridge is too high, though, the sound may become a little hollow (and the instrument will be hard to play because of the extra string height).

THE SOUND POST

Inside the body, under the bridge, is the sound post. This thin, round spruce stick is not just there for strength: it also has a lot to do with the sound. French violin makers even call it *l'âme*: the 'soul' of the instrument.

Position

The sound post must be straight, and long enough to be firmly wedged between the top and the back, but not so long that it pushes the two apart. The exact position is also critical, and measured to under a twentieth of an inch.

Adjustment

A violin maker can adjust the sound of a cello by moving the sound post a fraction. In this way the sound can be made slightly less edgy, for example, or a little brighter. Also, if one string sounds louder or softer than the others, repositioning the sound post can be a solution (so can using different strings, as is explained in Chapter 6).

PEGS AND FINE TUNERS

You can tune a cello with the wooden tuning pegs at the top. If you play steel strings, you will have to use the fine tuners in the tailpiece as well. Both pegs and fine tuners come in different types and sizes.

Ebony, rosewood, boxwood

Pegs get thicker toward their round heads (or *thumb pieces*), and this tapered shape prevents them from twisting loose by themselves. They are usually made of ebony, which is also used for tailpieces, though rosewood and boxwood are popular, too. Rosewood has a reddish-brown colour, and boxwood is usually yellowish.

Damaged strings

If the wood of the pegs is too soft, the strings will soon wear grooves into them. These grooves, in turn, may damage the strings.

Parisian eyes

Pegs come in various different designs. One popular choice

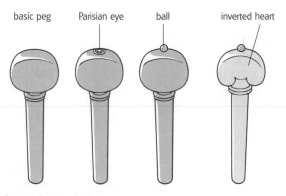

basic peg   Parisian eye   ball   inverted heart

Various tuning-peg designs

is the inverted heart with a ball on top, and another is the *Parisian eye*, a small mother-of-pearl dot with a metal ring around it. A simple mother-of-pearl dot is called an *eye*, a *single eye* or an *eyelet*.

A good fit
Cheap cellos are often hard to tune, or they go out of tune quickly, because the pegs are of poor quality or haven't been properly custom-fitted to the instrument.

Removable pegs
Depending on your posture and the way you hold the cello, the tuning pegs of the C- and G-strings may bother you. To solve that problem, you can have tuning pegs with a removable thumb piece installed. Once the strings have been tuned, you can simply take out the thumb piece.

Fine tuners
Steel-core strings respond so much to changes of tension that tuning them with the big tuning pegs can be problematic, so fine tuners are used to get the strings to their exact pitches. These fine tuners, which are usually built into the tailpiece, are also known by various other names, including *adjusters*, *tuning* or *string adjusters*, and *string tuners*.

Separate fine tuners
You can buy fine tuners separately, usually for around £5–10 each. A tip: if your cello has a wooden tailpiece,

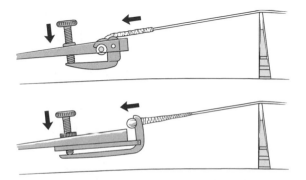

Built-in fine tuners (above) are smaller than the ones available separately (below)

which usually is quite heavy in itself, the added weight of the fine tuners may muffle the sound of your instrument (see page 41). If so, you may be better off buying a light-weight alloy or synthetic tailpiece with built-in fine tuners.

Geared pegs

Instead of fine tuners, you can get a special type of peg with a built-in gear system. For one full turn of the shaft of the peg, you have to turn the thumb piece a couple of times, rather than just once, allowing for much finer adjustment than a conventional peg. Another option, though very rare, is to use metal pegs with very thin shafts. And there are also cellos (mainly older ones) that have metal tuning mechanisms, called *machine heads*, similar to the ones found on double basses and bass guitars.

TAILPIECE

Tailpieces, believe it or not, may also influence the sound of your instrument, though you need to have a good instrument and be a good cellist to notice differences this subtle. Tailpieces come in various materials and designs, and with or without decoration or built-in fine tuners.

French or Hill

There are a great variety of tailpiece models available. Two examples of well-known basic designs are the *French model*, with a very slim upper part, or the *Hill model*, named after a British manufacturer, with elegant lines and

A French model tailpiece ...

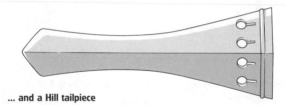

... and a Hill tailpiece

an angular end. Some tailpieces are available with a Parisian eye or other inlaid decorations.

Parallel

The strings should always run parallel between the bridge and the tailpiece. If they don't, the tailpiece may be too narrow or too wide for the instrument.

The sound

The weight of a tailpiece can affect the sound of a cello in a similar way to the weight of the bridge. A heavy wooden tailpiece can slightly muffle the tone, making it a little less bright. A lighter (alloy or synthetic) tailpiece gives a clearer, brighter sound, but can also make the tone a bit uncentred.

All together

These differences in tone are not usually very obvious, but the combined mass of a heavy wooden tailpiece with four big fine tuners can make for a noticeably duller tone, especially if the tailpiece is too close to the bridge (see page 95).

Tailpiece loop

Traditionally, the tailpiece loop or *hanger* is made of gut, hence its other name, *tailgut*. There are cellists who feel even this enhances the sound of the instrument, but most tailpieces are attached with an adjustable synthetic cord, which is more reliable and cheaper, or with a steel wire. Gut does have a very attractive look, though, especially on an old instrument.

THE END PIN

The end pin doesn't do much more than support the instrument, but there are numerous variations in design.

The screw

A normal height adjustment screw on a plain steel end pin usually works just fine, but there are numerous anti-slip alternatives. An eye bolt may be used instead of a normal screw, for example, or the end pin may have a knurled surface or indentations (which can also be useful for remembering your preferred height setting).

Collar

A cello with a full ebony trim also has an ebony end button, but buttons can be made of other types of wood too. Some also have decorations, such as a gold-plated collar.

Hollow or solid

End pins can be hollow or solid, the latter simply being a little heavier. Most experts agree that the end pin does not influence the tone of the instrument, but some players do prefer hollow (or solid) rods for sound reasons. Some also favour wooden end pins, which have become quite rare, and others use a modern, lightweight carbon-fibre version. Comparing end pins and their effect on the sound of a cello is usually quite hard, not only because the differences are so subtle, but also because the fittings are not universal and replacing them often requires the instrument to be opened up.

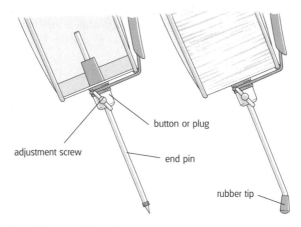

button or plug

adjustment screw

end pin

rubber tip

Two different end-pin designs

Bent end pins

Players who let their instrument lean very far backwards may benefit from a bent end pin – on some you can even adjust the angle. A less expensive solution is to use a end pin with a small bend at the very end.

Rubber tip

On most surfaces, the rubber tip at the end of the end pin won't keep the instrument from slipping away. If you take the tip off, you will usually find a sharp steel point, which works better on most wooden surfaces, but is quite likely to damage the floor.

Anchors

There are many devices available to stop your cello from sliding away from you as you play. With names like *end-pin anchors* or *spike holders*, they range from simple rubber balls and non-skid discs to holders that can be attached to the front legs of your chair with adjustable straps or cords (these are the most reliable and the only ones that work on all surfaces). Some players feel that the sound suffers from using an anchor, and prefer to play with the steel point stuck into a wooden stage, but they are very popular nonetheless. Prices range from around £5 to £30.

Height setting

The best height setting for your end pin depends on many factors, from your height and posture, to your seat and the angle at which you hold the cello. Most rods are adjustable from 14" to 20" (35–50cm) and they can be replaced by even longer ones. A rod that is too short can cause bad posture and back problems.

Cello chairs

The chair you use when playing the cello is very important for achieving a good posture, and this is something that you should discuss with your teacher. Children will need a lower-than-average chair, and players of all ages should use a sturdy seat that is either flat or slightly forward leaning – avoid chairs that wobble or lean backwards. Special cello chairs are available, but most players do without one.

TESTING TIPS

Going into a shop and trying out lots of cellos, one after the other, can be a bit overwhelming. Here are some tips to make testing and comparing more effective.

Take it with you

If you already have a cello, take it with you when you go to choose a new one – comparing it with other cellos may make it easier to judge what you hear. If you have your own bow, take that with you too, or use the best one available in the store, as a good bow will give you a much better idea of what the different cellos are capable of.

Someone else

If you haven't started playing cello yet, or you've only just begun, you won't know whether an instrument has a poor sound or whether it's just the way you're playing it. So ask someone who does play to demonstrate the different cellos to you, whether it's a salesperson or a teacher or friend you've brought along.

By ear

If you ask someone else to play, you can also hear how an instrument sounds from a distance, which will be quite different from having it right by your ear. And if you simply can't choose between a few instruments, you can compare their sounds without looking to see which is being played. This way you'll be choosing only by ear, without taking price, finish, manufacturer or age into account. You may find you prefer the sound of the cheapest of the bunch.

Very different

To get an idea of how cellos sound in the room you're in, you could start by playing two very different cellos – one with a bright sound and one with a mellow, dark sound. Having heard these extremes, you may also find it easier to judge the tone of any others you try.

Three by three

Instead of trying out lots of cellos one by one, work through the selection systematically. First take three and compare them with each other. Replace the one you like least and pick out another. Compare the three again – and so on.

Something simple

If you have a lot of cellos to choose from, it's often easier if you only play briefly on each one. Play something simple, so that you can concentrate on the instrument rather than what you're playing – even a scale will do. However, once you've narrowed the selection down to just a few, you'll probably want to play longer and more demanding pieces on each, so you can get to know the instruments better.

String by string

You can also compare cellos string by string and note by note. How do the open strings sound, for example, or notes played in the highest positions? Is there a good balance between the volume of the strings in all positions? How is the tone when you pluck the strings, or when you play long notes?

Same pitch, same strings

The cellos that you are comparing must be tuned properly and to the same pitch. Otherwise, one instrument might sound a little warmer than the others, say, just because it's tuned a bit lower. For similar reasons, the cellos should all really have the same or similar strings. If they don't, you will be comparing the strings as well as just the cellos.

LISTENING TIPS

Comparing the sounds of cellos is something you have to learn how to do – the more often you do it, the more subtle differences you'll hear. First, though, you need to know what kind of things to listen out for. Here are some tips.

Projection and volume

Some cellos will always sound very soft or weak, however energetically they are played. If you use such an instrument in an orchestra, no one will be able to hear you. Other cellos can be heard quite clearly, in big spaces and among other instruments, even when you play quite softly. A cello like this is said to have good *projection*. Of course, cellos also differ in the volume level they can produce: some just sound louder than others.

Balance

The four strings of a cello not only sound different in pitch but also in tone, or *timbre*. If you play an A on the open A-string, for example, and then play the same pitch on the D- and G-strings, you'll hear the same note with three very different timbres. Cellists usually want their low strings to sound warm and dark and their higher strings to be brilliant and bright, but for everything to sound balanced at the same time. If the strings sound too differ-ent, you won't be able to make a smooth transition from one to the other.

Response and depth of sound

A cello should have a good response, even when you play very softly. If not, the instrument will be harder to play, and you'll have to really work to produce each note. Also, on a cello with a poor response, every time you play a note it takes a tiny bit longer to achieve a full sound. The C-string is the most critical one when it comes to response, as it's so heavy. It's also the string that is most likely to lack depth of sound, followed by its neighbour, the G.

An uncentred tone

On some cellos, the tone never really seems to get there: the instrument lacks foundation, producing an uncentred, weak timbre. However, bear in mind that an uncentred tone – and a slow response – isn't always down to the instrument. The strings, the bow, the rosin and the way the cello is played are all significant factors, too.

Dynamics and colours

A good cello will produce a pleasing tone over a big dynamic range – whether played very softly or very loudly. It should also allow you to produce different timbres and tone colours easily. For example, if you bow the strings a little closer to the fingerboard, the sound should become noticeably rounder than if you play close to the bridge (*sul ponticello*). Ideally, the instrument should sound good both ways, leaving you plenty of room to colour the sound.

Richer

The better an instrument is, the richer it sounds. Richer means a beautiful, resonant, full-throated tone; it means there's more of everything; and it means that you can produce a wide variety of tonal colours.

Poorer

Poorer-sounding instruments are often described as nasal (it sounds like it has a cold), hollow (like you're playing in a bathroom), thin (as if it's a miniature cello), or dull (as if there's a blanket over it) – and everybody has more or less the same idea of what those words mean.

Opinions, opinions

Apart from the things described above, a good sound is mostly a matter of personal preference. Bear in mind that when two people listen to the same instrument they may use very different words to describe what they hear. What one finds harsh or edgy (and therefore unpleasant), someone else may describe as bright and clear (and therefore pleasant), and what's warm to one ear sounds dull to another.

USED CELLOS

When you go to buy a used instrument, there are a few extra things you should bear in mind.

Repairs

First of all: no matter what's broken, a decent cello can almost always be fixed. But if you decide to buy an instrument that requires some work, you need to know what it's going to cost first. Further, whilst some types of damage are easy to see, other kinds only an expert will spot. If in doubt, take a cello for appraisal before buying it (see also page 23).

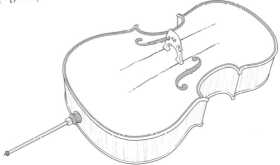

Major damage: cracks in the sound-post and bass-bar areas

Things to check

A complete list of everything you could check when examining an secondhand cello is beyond the scope of this book, but here are some of the most important.

- **Varnish wear**. One place to check is where your left hand touches the body. If the varnish has completely gone, you may need to have something done about it.
- If the type of varnish allows for it, it is usually **touched up** after repairs (see page 27). Check that this has been done properly.
- Check the **edges** as this is where cellos receive most of their knocks. Repairing damaged edges can cost a lot of money.
- Cracks in the top or the back always run lengthways. Cracks by **the sound post and the bass bar** are often hard to see and even harder to repair.
- Other places to check for cracks include **the heel of the neck, and the cheeks** (sides) of the pegbox near the pegs.
- If **the tuning pegs** are pushed very far into the pegbox, sticking way out at the other end, they may need to be replaced, and the holes may need to be *rebushed* (lined), which is quite an expensive job.
- Glue can come loose along the edges, for instance, or at the neck. Two ways to discover **loose glue joints** are to play the instrument and to gently tap it all around the body.

Cracks in the cheeks and the heel of the neck

Woodworm

Woodworm burrow into wood and leave narrow tunnels. This can be very serious in string instruments, especially if they attack the top or back. You won't find woodworm in a cello that has always been played – this particular creature doesn't like music – but you may come across the problem on older instruments, or instruments that have been left lying around for long periods. If you want to know whether they're still around, lay the cello on a piece of black cardboard overnight. If there's sawdust on the cardboard the next day, the cello is inhabited.

6. GOOD STRINGS

The type of strings you use greatly influences your sound. You can choose between dozens of types and brands, with different core materials and windings. Every type of string has its own timbre, some are easier to play than others, and some are more suited to some cellos than others.

Cello strings can last a long time – up to a year, or even longer. It does help, though, if they are fitted properly and kept clean. For more on keeping your strings in good condition, turn to Chapter 10, *Cello Maintenance*.

Steel, gut, synthetic

There are three main types of strings. First, there are those with a steel core, the most popular choice today. Second, there are gut strings, the original type, which sound a lot warmer and darker than steel. Lastly, there are strings with a synthetic core, which have a sound somewhere between the other two types.

Winding

Almost all cello strings are wound with ultra-thin metal ribbon. If not, they would have to be very thick in order to produce the desired pitches – and thick strings do not respond very well. The exact type of winding is very important to the way the strings sound and respond.

Wound with ultra-thin metal ribbon

Important

Strings are so important for how you sound and play that the difference between using cheap and expensive strings is often much bigger and more noticeable than the difference between using a cheaper and a more expensive cello. If you can afford it, it really is worth experimenting with different types of strings, though bear in mind that changing from steel to synthetic or gut strings will require you to adapt your technique, and possibly take extra lessons from a teacher who plays those types of strings. Your instrument will probably need to be adapted too (see page 93).

STEEL STRINGS

Steel strings offer a clear, bright, powerful sound and an immediate response. Also, they're very reliable and they last a long time, typically from six months to a year, or even longer.

The core

Steel strings come in two basic variations: with a solid core or with a core made up of a number of very thin steel strands. Solid (or *full-core*) strings have the brightest sound, whilst multi-strand (or *spiral-core*) strings are more flexible and produce a darker, fuller tone.

Combinations

Many cellists combine both types of steel strings on their instrument, using solid-core A- and D-strings for radiant, bright highs, and multi-strand G- and C-strings for warm, full-sounding lows. Some players use other combinations, such as a mixture of synthetic and steel strings (see page 52). Such 'custom sets' are readily available from some shops, but you can make up your own combination as well, of course.

The price

Most cheap cellos have steel strings, one reason being that they're relatively inexpensive – you can pick up a set of four for about £50 or even less. However, a set of professional-quality steel strings is usually around £100 or more, and there are even C-strings which retail for more than £75.

GUT STRINGS

The first cellos had sheep-gut strings, and some professional musicians still feel that this is the only type of string that can really bring out the instrument's beauty.

Sound

The sound of gut strings is often described as mellow, warm and rich. These strings allow for great variation in colour and inflection, though this in turn demands a good cellist and a good cello, too. Players who specialize in Baroque music (see page 34) often choose gut strings, either to get closer to the sound that would have been heard during the period or because they feel that their warm and gentle tone is well suited to the music. Such strings are sometimes wound with round wire (*roundwound*), like in the Baroque era, rather than with a flat ribbon. Some Baroque players use unwound (*plain*) D- and A-strings.

A few hours

Unlike steel strings, gut strings need to be broken in: it takes a few hours of playing to get them to develop their full sound. Because they stretch quite a lot when new, they also have to be tuned quite often at first. Additional tuning is also required, as gut strings detune with changes in temperature or humidity.

Expensive

Gut strings are an expensive option. A set costs in the region of £75–150, and they don't last as long as other types of strings, so you need to replace them more often. For this reason, some cellists use a gut A-string only, combined with three synthetic-core strings.

SYNTHETIC STRINGS

Synthetic-core strings lie somewhere between gut and steel, in terms of sound, ease of playing, life expectancy and price. A set of four typically costs about £75–100, though you can spend more.

Sound

Synthetic-core strings come with a wide variety of different materials and windings, so they vary considerably in terms of sound. Generally speaking, though, their tone is close to that of gut strings, but a bit brighter and louder.

Best of both worlds

Synthetic-core strings can be a good solution for players who want some of the advantages of gut strings but not all the disadvantages. They can also be combined with other types of strings, of course. One popular combination is to use synthetic-core strings for the C and the G, and steel for the other two.

Breaking them in

Just like gut strings, synthetic-core strings may only start to sound their best after they are played for a few hours. When they are brand-new, they can sound a little raw or harsh.

WINDINGS

String manufacturers use various types of windings, each of which makes for a different sound and feel. To create a particular balance between the four strings, they may even use different winding materials within one set, and strings can also have more than one winding.

Nickel or chrome

Generally speaking, a nickel winding will make for a rather soft, sweet or warm sound. Chromium or chrome-alloy windings, on the other hand, add brightness to the sound, and enhance the projection of the instrument.

Silver, aluminium and tungsten

A silver winding adds warmth and power to the lower strings. Silver-wound lower strings are often combined with aluminium-wound treble strings, the lighter metal providing extra clarity in the higher ranges. Tungsten is sometimes used instead of, or in combination with, silver. This dense material allows for even thinner low strings, which enhances their response. Tungsten may also help to avoid wolf notes (see page 74).

Other metals

Other materials used to wind strings include copper, tita-nium and silver mixed with gold. If you are looking for a particular sound, a good salesperson or violin maker will be able to help you with your choice. But if you really want to be sure, you'll need to try out different strings for yourself.

Discolour
Depending on the chemical makeup of your perspiration, you may find that silver and aluminium windings discolour very fast. If so, the only solution is to try out other types of windings.

LOUD OR SOFT
Synthetic and steel strings often come in several varieties, such as *dolce* (soft), *medium* and *forte* (strong). You may also see German descriptions like *weich* (soft) and *stark* (strong). Forte strings, also sometimes labelled *orchestra* or *solo,* are heavier than dolce strings.

Different tensions
Some string manufacturers describe their products in terms of tension, marketing low-, medium and high-tension strings. Usually, the higher the tension, the thicker the string's width, or *gauge*. High-tension strings take a little more effort to play and they respond slower than low-tension versions, but their brighter, stronger sound can enhance a cello's projection. Medium-tension strings are the most commonly used, and low-tension strings are often recommended for old instruments.

Right for the cello
Choosing the right type of strings is not just down to the sound and playability usually associated with them, but also to the specific instrument they will be used on. Using forte strings may work well on one cello, but their higher tension may actually reduce the sound on another instrument, for example.

Colours
To indicate the different types of strings, manufacturers use coloured thread at one of the string's ends. At the other end, the string's pitch is marked with another colour, to prevent you from putting the D-string where the A-string should be, and so on.

Confusing

Unfortunately, no uniform colour codes are used, so the same colour may mean one thing for one make and something else for another. Similarly, there's no consistency in what (string type or pitch) is indicated at which end of the string.

Same make and series

If the strings on a cello are of the same make and series, you will see four different colours (one for each pitch) at one end, and only one colour (for the series or type) at the other.

Mixed up

If this is not the case, there's a fair chance that the strings are of different brands, series or tensions, either deliberately or inadvertently. If the strings sound good together, that's no problem. If you want to know exactly which strings are fitted to your instrument, ask an expert, who will be able to tell from the colour codes.

Thick or thin

Gut strings come in different gauges. Heavier-gauge strings are harder work to play and don't respond as easily, but they usually sound fuller, louder and clearer.

Inches and millimetres

If you want to know exactly how thick a gut string is in inches, you have to divide its gauge by 500. For example, the width of a 14-gauge string is $14 \div 500 = 0.028''$. To get the width in millimetres, divide the gauge by 20.

String height

If you put higher-tension strings on your instrument, it may be that they end up further from the fingerboard, as they increase the tension on the neck. Conversely, lower-tension strings may decrease the instrument's string height. Adjusting string height is a job for a professional.

AND MORE

If you're putting new strings on your cello, you can make a note of their brand and type on pages 128–129 of this book.

Then you'll be able to buy the same type if you like them, or avoid them if you don't. This can be especially helpful if you mix and match string sets yourself. The more you know about the strings you use, the better you'll be able to adjust the sound of your instrument to your taste.

When to replace?

How long cello strings last depends on many things – how often you play, of course, but also on the core material of the strings, the type of winding, and on how well you keep them clean (see page 84). A tip: if the tension on a string is suddenly released, for instance because of an ill-fitting tuning peg or a sudden change in air humidity (see page 97), the winding may be damaged or the string may break whilst you're tuning it back up.

A year

If you have steel strings and you play for a few hours a week, you could try fitting new strings after a year or so. If the difference is very obvious, you may want to replace them sooner next time; but if you can't hear much change, you could wait longer. Steel strings usually last longer then synthetic strings, and gut strings wear out the quickest.

Short and dull

When plucking your strings only produces a short, dull tone, it's a sign that they are wearing out. Discolouring is another sign that the strings may be ready to be replaced, though silver-wound and aluminium-wound strings may still sound fine long after they have begun to discolour.

Damaged windings

A damaged winding often renders a string unplayable. You can prevent this from happening by making sure the grooves in the bridge and nut are wide enough for the strings you use (have them checked when you change to thicker strings), and by 'lubricating' the grooves from time to time by rubbing them with a soft lead pencil point.

Sleeves

Some strings come with short sleeves, designed to protect the winding at the bridge. If you choose to use them, make sure that most of the sleeve is on the side of the tailpiece;

otherwise it will muffle the sound too much. If muffling an overly bright string is exactly what you want to do, there are more effective devices available (see page 74).

Parchment
To prevent the thin A-string from cutting into the bridge, some bridges have a ebony or bone insert at that point, and violin makers often glue a tiny piece of vellum (parchment) under the string.

Fractional sizes
Special fractional-sized strings are available for smaller cellos, though the selection is quite limited. Some full-size strings are unsuitable for use on fractional instruments – they will make a weak tone and break easily – but others work perfectly well, and in some cases actually sound better than fractional-sized strings. It depends on both the instrument and the strings.

String brands
There are numerous string brands on the market, and many of them offer various types of cello strings. D'Addario, Pirastro, Super-Sensitive and Thomastik are some of the bigger companies, and cello (and other) strings are also made by Corelli, Jargar and Larsen, as well as by Dogal, Meisel, Pinnacle, Prim, Pyramid, Savarez, Stellar, Supreme and Syntha-Core. Some of these companies also make rosin, other accessories or even instruments.

7. BOWS AND ROSINS

You'll only get the very best from your cello if you have a bow that suits your instrument, your technique and the music you play. This chapter tells you what you need to know, covering woods, frogs, ferrules, hair, weight, balance and rosin.

The stick of a bow can be made of wood or a synthetic material, with wood still being the most popular choice. Most cheaper wooden bows are made of brazilwood, while more expensive bows are usually pernambuco.

Brazilwood and pernambuco

Though they start pretty cheap, you should expect to pay around £150–300 for a decent brazilwood bow. If you pay more, you'll probably get one with a stick made of pernambuco, which is slightly reddish in colour. Pernambuco bows can last more than a hundred years without losing their elasticity.

Overlap

So, if you intend to spend about £300 on a bow, you could choose either an 'expensive' brazilwood model or an 'inexpensive' pernambuco one. You should choose the one that suits you and your instrument best, whatever wood it's made of.

Other woods

Though brazilwood and pernambuco are the most common, you may come across bows in other woods. Snakewood, for example, a dense expensive wood with an appearance similar to snakeskin, is sometimes used for special Baroque bows.

Synthetic bows

Some bows have a synthetic stick, made of carbon fibre or fibreglass, for example. The cheapest models, available for £35 or less, are designed for children. They're very durable and don't need much care or attention. However, professional synthetic bows are also available, and they can cost thousands of pounds.

Synthetic hair

The very cheapest bows often come with synthetic hair. This provides less grip than traditional horsehair, and never allows a cello to sound its best.

Bleaching

Some manufacturers bleach bow hair to make it look bright and white. However, this strongly reduces the durability of the hair.

The mountings

A bow's *mountings* are its metal parts, such as the screw button, the *back plate* of the frog, and the *ferrule* or *D-ring*, where the bow hair enters the frog. The material used for the mountings gives a very rough indication of the price range and quality of the bow.

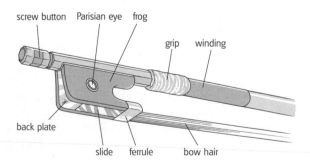

Silver, gold and nickel silver

Silver-mounted bows usually start at around £350, and gold-mounted bows, which are pretty rare, may cost five times as much. Most cheaper bows have nickel-silver mountings.

Contrary to what you might expect, nickel silver does not actually contain any silver.

Full-lined
The picture opposite shows a full-lined frog. Inexpensive bows often have a half-lined frog, which lacks the back plate behind the slide.

CLOSE UP
Of course, there is more to a bow than the material used for the stick and mountings. Here are some other things to look out for.

Eight-sided or round
The stick (or *bowstick*), which gets gradually thinner from the frog to the head, can be round or octagonal (eight-sided). Some cellists feel that an octagonal stick makes a bow play better, as it may be a little stiffer and more stable than a round stick.

A little more
A bow with an octagonal stick usually costs a little more – not because it's necessarily better, but simply because it takes longer to make one.

Frog
The frog is usually made of ebony, but cheap bows often have plastic frogs. And there are differences in terms of decoration, too. The slide, at the bottom of the frog, generally has a mother-of-pearl finish, and the frog itself may be decorated with single or Parisian eyes. Intricately carved and elaborately decorated models are also available.

Screw buttons
Screw buttons, also known as *end screws* or *adjusters*, come in two- and three-part versions (silver-ebony and silver-ebony-silver respectively), and some have an eye on each of their eight sides.

Branded name
Usually the name of the bow maker or the bow's brand is literally branded into the stick, just above the frog.

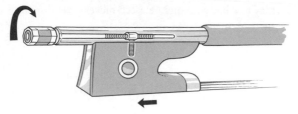

Tightening the bow hair: the frog moves backward

Bow grip

The leather bow grip or *thumb grip* may be a little thinner on one stick than the next, and occasionally it has tiny 'ventilation holes'. On inexpensive bows, vinyl is some-times used instead of leather, and this may feel a little sticky when you play. If the bow grip feels too thin, you can install a thumb cushion, which simply slides over it. If it's too thick, its best to ask a professional to replace it.

Winding or lapping

Silver thread is usually used for the winding or *lapping*. Some bows have a silk winding or a synthetic imitation *baleen* (whalebone) winding in one or two colours. The use of real baleen has been banned.

Face

In the past, the protective *face* at the other end of the stick was often made of ivory. Today, bow makers use a synthetic material, metal or bone.

CHOOSING BOWS

When given the choice between a great instrument and a decent bow, and a decent instrument and a great bow, most professional cellists would go for the latter. Some cel-lists even say your bow should cost as much as your cello, though others say you should spend half as much, or a quarter – so don't take too much notice of rules like this. The best bow for you is the one in your price range that you feel most comfortable with and the one that helps you to make your instrument sound its best.

The best bow?

The type of bow that will suit you best depends on your

bowing technique and on the music you play. But a bow also must suit your instrument and the strings you use – so always try out bows with your own instrument.

A selection
Because a bow should suit the style of music you play, cellists often have a selection of bows. That way, they can choose one bow for when a bright, clear tone is desired, for example, and another for when the music demands a more mellow timbre.

More expensive
A more expensive bow is not always better. An antique bow, for example, will often cost a lot more than an equally good new one (see page 64). You may even get lucky and find a great bow for a bargain price – even some top cellists have a 'cheap' bow in their collection because it happens to be perfect for certain pieces of music.

Three by three
As with cellos, the best way to test a wide selection of bows isn't to try them all one after the other – you will probably have forgotten what the first one sounded and felt like by the time you reach the last one. Instead, concentrate on just two or three bows at a time. Compare them, reject the one you like least, pick out another, and so on.

Hair tension
When comparing bows, take the hair tension into account. The 'best' tension may vary per bow, depending on the elasticity of the stick among other things. As a starting point, you may want to check the distance between the middle of the stick and the hair. When this gets to around 0.4" (1cm), the tension will usually be set about right, unless the stick has an unusual taper.

Number of turns
Turning the screw button a set number of times for each bow isn't a good starting point, as this will probably result in different hair tensions on each. A tip: the number of times you turn the adjustment screw may even vary on your own bow from time to time, depending on humidity and temperature. When the air is very dry, for example,

the stick will be slightly stiffer so you'll need to put less tension on the hair.

What to play?

Of course, the best test for any bow is to play the music you intend to use it for. Try out all the bowing styles you know. Play slowly, fast, loudly and softly, play staccato and legato, and keep listening and feeling to how the bow performs. Some bows respond better to the way you play and to exactly where you bow the strings than others.

Sound

A different bow will make you sound different, just like another instrument. These nuances will usually come out best if you play slow phrases, and you'll hear more of them when testing bows in the higher price ranges (and when using a good cello).

Curved

A bow should be curved so that the hair, when slack, just touches the stick. If the stick is more curved than that, the hair may touch it when playing, and the bow may also feel a little jumpy. On the other hand, if the stick is too straight, it may feel a bit sluggish. Looking on the bright side, you could also say that a more curved bow is good for *spiccato* (in which the bow lightly bounces off the strings), while a fairly straight bow would be better for slower phrases. But then a really good bow should allow you to play anything.

Flexibility

To check the flexibility of a bow, you can rest its face on a table and gently push it downwards in the middle with your forefinger. With a stiffer bow it's often easier to play fast, but with a flexible bow it's usually easier to produce a good, even tone. Again, a good bow should allow you to do both. A tip: there are synthetic bows whose flexibility can be adjusted to match your technique or the music you play.

Weight

A full-sized bow usually weighs between 2.2 and 2.4 ounces (78–85 grams), and generally a weight of about 2.3 ounces is recommended. If you're looking for quite a full-bodied sound, you may want to find a relatively heavy bow. Lighter bows are better suited for a lighter sound, though if a bow is too light it won't make the strings vibrate enough and you won't produce much sound at all.

Small differences
Even the smallest weight differences can influence how you sound and play – and some cellists can spot the tiniest weight differences between two bows.

Balance
The balance of a bow is also very important. If a bow is heavier at the head end, it will feel heavier but may well be easier to guide. And a bow with the weight further back will feel lighter but require more careful guidance. To compare bows in this respect, you can carefully balance them on your forefinger about 9–9.5" (22–24cm) from the end of the stick (not including the screw button). A bow's balance can be adapted by using more or less thread for the winding, for example, or even by making the tip heavier.

Response
With some bows, the tone builds up very gently and gradually, and with others the strings respond very quickly. To check the response of a bow, play lots of short notes on the lowest strings. Most cellists like to have a bow with an even response – in other words, a bow that produces the same response from the strings in the middle, near the head and near the frog.

In line
When testing a bow, look along its back, from the frog, to check that it is straight. Just like a cello neck, the bow must not look twisted or uneven.

All different
There are even small differences between every two bows of the same brand and series, so always buy the one you tested rather than an 'identical' one from the storeroom.

Secondhand bows
If you are planning to buy a used bow, bear the following points in mind:

- If the hair is overstretched, a bow will feel very sluggish. The solution is to have the bow **rehaired** (see page 88).
- Another problem with overstretched bow hair is that the frog needs to be shifted very far back. This changes **the balance of the stick**.
- A bow can **lose some of its curve** over the years. It may be possible to restore it, but be sure you know whether the bow is worth the expense.
- What Stradivarius is to the cello, **François Tourte** (France, 1747–1835) is to the bow. If you find his name on a bow, it probably won't be a real Tourte, unless the price is in the region of £25,000.

Brands

A few well-known bow brands are Arcos Brasil, Ary-France, Dörfler, Höfner, Paesold, Seifert, Student Arpège, Roger, Werner, and W.R. Schuster. Low-cost synthetic bows are made by Glasser, amongst other companies, and Berg, Coda and Spiccato produce more expensive synthetic bows.

Workshop and master bows

There are also dozens of small bow workshops around, especially in Germany and France. Bows by independent makers, who work alone, usually start at around £750 and go up to ten times that, though some small workshops also produce bows in the lower price ranges. If a bow doesn't have a brand name at all, it's probably a very cheap one.

ROSIN

Rosin makes the bow hair slightly sticky. When you play, this stickiness causes the bow to 'grip' the stings for a fraction of a second, until the tension gets too high and the strings slip. This *stick-slip motion* is repeated over and over again as you draw the bow over the strings, causing the vibrations that produce the sound.

Hard

Pieces of rosin, sometimes called *rosin cakes*, generally cost around £3–10, and they come in cloths or boxes so you're less likely to touch them. As a rule, a piece of rosin should last a year or longer, though it's quite hard and brittle stuff, so if you drop it there's a good chance it will break.

Light and dark

Many brands sell rosins in two colours at the same price: one light and honey-coloured, the other dark and almost liquorice-like in colour. It's often said that light rosins are harder and less sticky, which makes them good for use in hot conditions, such as in the summer, as higher temperatures make them softer. This is true of some brands, but it can also be the other way around. Often, only the colour is different (and even that vanishes when you start playing, as rosin dust is always white).

Rosin is sold in cloths and boxes, rectangular or round blocks, and in various colours

Harder and softer

The rosin of one brand may be harder than that of another, and some brands sell rosin in various hardnesses. You can sometimes feel the difference between the softer and harder rosins by pressing your nail into them, but often the difference is quite subtle.

Response and noise

It is often said that softer rosin makes your strings respond better, especially if you use gut strings, which don't suit very hard rosin. However, softer rosin is also stickier, so may increase the number of unwanted noises, especially on non-steel strings.

Loud and quiet

Some experts – cellists as well as rosin makers – claim that harder rosins are especially suitable for louder music, for when a fast response is required, and for when the music you play requires a lot of bow pressure. But other experts recommend harder rosin for quiet pieces, because it's less sticky and will therefore produce less unwanted noise.

Sticky

An extra-sticky rosin tends to produce less dust, so less gets onto your cello. What's more, you won't need to apply as much pressure on your bow. On the other hand, this type of rosin is more likely to clog up your bow hair, so you will need to have it cleaned more often. Some more expensive rosins, having finer particles, are said to produce more, and finer, dust.

Gold and silver

Some rosins contain gold or silver particles, at not too much extra cost. These precious metals are said to add clarity and brightness to the sound, though not all cellists can tell the difference.

Barely noticeable

Many experts believe that the biggest difference between most rosins is the amount of dust they produce during application and just afterwards, claiming that once you're playing the differences are barely noticeable, if at all. Most experts agree, however, that if you're using a very high-quality bow, any differences are pronounced.

Confusing

Just to add to the confusion, the very same rosin is sometimes sold by more than one brand, with a different package, label, price and description. And, while some manufacturers sell different rosins for cello, violin and viola, others make just one for all three instruments.

The best rosin?

You will probably hear all sorts of contradictory opinions about which types of rosin are best and what the differences between them are. It's best to take such information with a pinch of salt, as even experts don't agree on most of the issues. The differences are usually quite slim, and ultimately the only way to find the best rosin is to experiment with different types and brands on your own bow, cello and strings.

New bow or strings

If you buy a new bow you may well need a different rosin to do it justice, and the same is true if you start using a different type of strings. Some manufacturers try to make it easier for you to match the right strings with the right rosin by producing a rosin with the same name as each of their string series. This can be useful, though it doesn't mean that it isn't worth experimenting with other brands and types, too.

Hours

Unfortunately, trying out rosins is a slow process – the old rosin will still be effective for a good few hours of playing after you've applied a new one. That's why cellists who regularly use different rosins for different styles of music generally use them on different bows.

Allergies

Some people are allergic to traditional rosin, but special hypoallergenic versions are available. Rosins that produce less dust may also help.

8. ACCESSORIES

If you buy just a cello, rather than a complete outfit, you'll need to invest in a gig bag or a case to protect it. And there are numerous other cello accessories available, including stands, mutes and devices to suppress the stuttering sound of wolf notes.

Cello bags and cases are available in a wide variety of styles and prices, the most expensive case costing at least twenty times as much as the cheapest bag. Bags are usually easier to carry around than cases, as they're softer and lighter, and usually come with adjustable padded backpack straps. However, a good case offers much better protection.

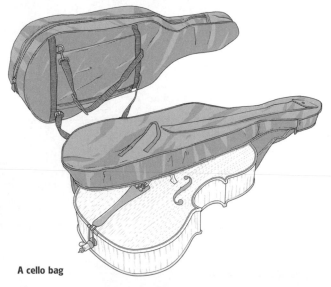

A cello bag

Cello bags

The cheapest cello bags are available for about £30, but prices go up to around four times that. The price depends largely on the quality and thickness of the padding – from none to an inch (2.5cm) or more – and the quality of the bag itself. For example, 600 denier nylon is denser and stronger than 420 denier nylon.

Pockets

Cello bags usually have pockets for one or more bows and spare strings, and sometimes for sheet music and more. A tip: to avoid damaging your bow, always remove it from the bag before unpacking the cello. And if you want to keep the inside of the bow pocket clean from rosin, put the bow in a separate washable cotton bag first, or simply wrap it a section of old cotton bed sheet.

Cases

Hard cello cases have shell made of plywood, fibreglass or a synthetic material (such as thermoplastic or ABS), covered in vinyl, leather, or nylon or cordura cloth. Prices start at around £200, though cheaper models are sometimes available, and go up to around to £600 or more. A good case

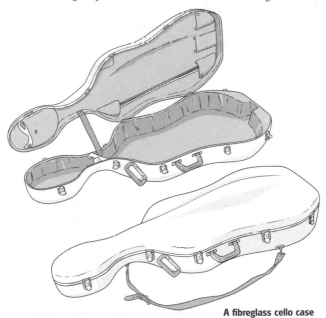

A fibreglass cello case

will absorb the shock if it falls over, and will be sturdy enough to resist being crushed if something heavy falls on it. The cheapest cases are less strong and may not offer enough protection.

Inside

A padded, lined interior absorbs shocks and prevents scratches. Generally the padding is thicker and of higher quality in more expensive cases. If a choice between a velour or velvet lining is offered, the latter will cost a little extra.

Suspension cases

In some cases, the instrument is suspended, meaning there are cavities below or above certain sections of the instrument, such as the back and scroll.

Bow holders

The inside of the lid usually has holders or trays for two or sometimes three bows. A tip: always put the bows in with their hair facing outwards. Many bow holders have a ribbon underneath, preventing the lining from being damaged by rosin. Sometimes it is removable, and so can be washed, but not in most cases. You can also get separate cases for one or more bows, which are useful if you have more bows than your cello case can accommodate.

Protective cloth

Covering a cello with a cloth before closing the case offers extra protection against damage and dirt from the bow(s). Some cases come with a cloth or a foam pad specifically for this purpose.

Case covers

A good case should close tightly enough so that your instrument won't get wet if it rains. For extra protection, though, you may want to invest in a separate case cover. They are available with or without extra padding and pockets for music and more.

Locks and hinges

Most cases are lockable. This is mainly to ensure that the catches cannot open by accident if the case gets dropped, for example, so make it a habit to lock them. When choosing a case, check the locks, hinges, handles and carrying straps carefully: these are often the weak spots.

Handles, wheels and feet

Cases and bags often have two or even three handles, making it easier take the instrument out of a car and so on. Some models also come with removable wheels, though it's not advisable to use these on anything other than even, smooth floors. To protect against wear, some cases and bags have rubber or metal feet on the bottom and the sides.

Hygrometer

Cellos are particularly sensitive to very dry air. Some of the more expensive cases available have a built-in hygrometer, so you can check humidity at any time (see pages 97–98).

Cello stands

It's safest to keep your instrument in its case or bag when you're not playing. Especially for short breaks, though, some players like to use a cello stand, to avoid having to lay the instrument on the floor. Collapsible cello stands, which usually also have a holder for a bow, are available from around £30. Beware, though, that the rubber pads on some stands leave imprints in the cello's varnish, especially in warm weather. For home use, you can also get more expensive padded, box-shaped stands, but these aren't portable. A tip: if you don't use a stand and you need to lay your cello down for a minute, always put it on its side, never on its back or top.

A cello stand

MUTES

A *mute* is a little device that can be slotted onto the bridge of a string instrument to make the sound softer, mellower or warmer. They work by muffling some of the higher frequencies of the sound. If a composer wants you to use a mute, the instruction 'with mute' will be written on the music, usually in Italian: *con sordino*. Practice mutes (see page 16) muffle the sound a lot more than regular mutes.

Bigger and heavier

As discussed on pages 35–36, a heavy bridge can slightly muffle the sound of a cello, and a mute works in basically the same way. It makes the bridge heavier and absorbs some of the vibrations, so fewer vibrations are transferred to the body to be amplified. The bigger or heavier a mute is, the more it will muffle the sound.

Tourte

Clothes pegs

You can demonstrate this with a couple of wooden clothes pegs. Very carefully attach one to the bridge of your cello and you'll hear that the sound has become slightly muffled. Attach another, doubling the added mass, and the muffling effect will be stronger.

Hill

Different types

Mutes come in rubber, metal or wood, and in a wide variety of designs. Most mutes are fairly inexpensive, costing between £3 and £10.

wire

Detachable or slide-on

The most basic mute looks like a thick three-pronged comb, and is only put onto the cello when it is needed. Another type, the *fixed mute* or *slide-on mute*, stays attached to your strings – if you don't need it, you simply slide it down to the tailpiece. Slide-on mutes come in rubber (the Tourte model) and wire versions.

ebony

Various types of mutes

Which is best?

Slide-on mutes are useful in pieces where you have to change quickly between playing with and without a mute. But there are some cellists who prefer never to use them, on the grounds that when they are down by the tailpiece they may either continue to muffle the sound a tiny bit (though you're unlikely to notice this) or rattle due to the vibrations of the strings. Others dislike clip-on mutes, because they are less convenient – and easy to lose.

A slide-on wire mute at the tailpiece ...

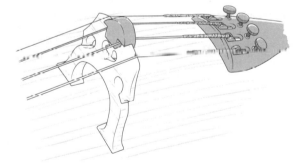

... and a slide-on rubber mute on the bridge

A sweeter tone

A wire mute can be used to make your sound just a tiny bit sweeter – simply slide it to a position somewhere between the bridge and the tailpiece. The closer you get to the bridge, the stronger the muffling effect will be. You can also set a wire mute diagonally, so that it muffles the high strings more than the low ones, or vice versa.

Tone filter

To slightly mute one or more particular strings, you can attach rubber sleeves around them, at the bridge. A faster solution is to use a small rubber disc, known as a *tone filter*, which can be put between the string and the bridge without removing the string.

Take it off

Always take mutes off your cello before packing it away. Small mutes like wire mutes can stay where they are, but bigger ones could cause damage to the instrument in transit.

WOLF NOTES

Many good cellos are plagued by *wolf notes*: at certain pitches the sound seems to stutter or howl. If you want to check a cello for wolf notes (or *wolfs*), play the notes D to F in the octave below middle C, on both on G- and C-strings. Occasionally, other pitches may produce wolf notes too, especially if you are bowing close to the bridge.

Spring-mounted weights

A wolf note is the result of part of the body vibrating at a speed which is very close to the vibrations of the note you are playing. To combat wolfs, you can have a special spring-mounted weight installed inside your cello, limiting the problematic vibrations.

Tubes

In some cases, wolfs can be eliminated by attaching a short metal tube to the problem string between the bridge and

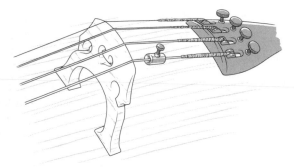

A metal-tube wolf note suppressor

the tailpiece – use trial and error to find the optimal position. These tubes are inexpensive and widely available.

Other solutions

Mild wolfs can also sometimes be suppressed by using a mute; by changing to a heavier or lighter bridge; by mounting a fractional-sized tailpiece; by choosing lower-tension strings; or by replacing chromium-wound strings by tungsten- or silver-wound strings. Putting a cork between the tailpiece and the top may work too (though this will also muffle your tone), and applying more pressure to the bow as you play can prevent a wolf from sounding.

How do they work?

When you play a note, the strings vibrate and they cause the body to do the same. However, like all objects, cello bodies naturally vibrate most easily at certain speeds (their *resonant frequencies*). If the strings are vibrating at a frequency very close to one of these speeds, the body will vibrate at a slightly different speed to the strings. The different vibrations interfere with each other and a wolf note occurs. The speed of the stuttering noise depends on the difference between the two speeds. If you play the E below middle C, for example, the string vibrates 165 times per second (165 hertz). If the instrument has a tendency to vibrate at, say, 160 hertz, the wolf will stutter five times per second (165 − 160 = 5).

Combating wolfs

Fighting wolfs is a matter of changing the resonant frequencies of the instrument, usually by adding weight (or by removing it, such as shortening the fingerboard). Sometimes a cello may develop wolf note problem after certain repairs have been carried out, such as having the bass bar replaced.

Fine instruments

Ironically, high-quality cellos are the ones that tend to suffer from wolf notes – cheap instruments are usually not resonant enough to create them.

9. TUNING

A cello has to be tuned before you can play it. When you start out, your teacher may help you, but sooner or later you'll have to learn to tune up yourself. It's not difficult, but it takes practice to become accurate and quick at it. This chapter covers some basic tuning techniques and offers tips and tricks for making tuning easier.

On a well-adjusted cello, steel or synthetic strings don't go out of tune very quickly. Even so, you always need to check the tuning before you start playing.

Steel strings and fine tuners
With steel strings, even the slightest rotation of a peg translates into a major difference in the tension on the string. That's why most steel-stringed cellos have fine tuners in the tailpiece (see page 39).

Pretuning
If you use steel strings, the tuning pegs are only used to 'pretune' the strings (get them roughly in tune). When doing this, make sure the fine tuners are in their middle settings, so you can use them to tune both up and down.

Plucking or bowing?
You can sound the string you are tuning by either bowing or plucking. Beginners often find plucking easier, but you can hear what you're doing better if you bow the strings.

The standard A
When you hear an orchestra or an ensemble tuning up,

their reference pitch is usually the A that you find to the right of middle C on a piano. It is sometimes referred to as a' or A4 (see page 11).

The A-string

The A-string of a cello sounds an octave lower than this: it is the A to the left of middle C, and is also known as a or A3. If you have a piano to hand, you can tune your A-string to this note.

Pianos and tuning forks

Often, though, there will be no piano around, in which case you'll need something else to provide a note to tune to. Most people use a tuning fork – a thick, two-pronged metal fork that you tap on your knee and hold by your ear to hear the note. Many electronic metronomes and tuners can also provide a note to tune to.

A tuning fork

An octave lower

Most tuning forks, metronomes and tuners produce the standard tuning pitch – a' – which is one octave higher than the cello A-string. This makes it a little more difficult to hear whether the A-string is tuned too high (*sharp*), too low (*flat*), or just right – especially if you are just learning to tune.

The same pitch

Comparing your A-string to the reference pitch is easier if you make the string sound exactly an octave higher. You can do this by playing the string while lightly touching it exactly midway, without pressing it against the finger-board. This will produce a clear, thin-toned note, called a *harmonic*, of the pitch a'. Learning to play harmonics takes a little practice, but it works really well.

Tuning the A-string

If the A on the cello sounds too low compared to your

reference pitch, simply increase the tension in the string by turning the fine tuner clockwise. And if it sounds too high, lower the tension by turning the fine tuner anti-clockwise. If you can't hear whether the string sounds flat or sharp, try turning the fine tuner all the way down, which should make it quite clearly flat. From there, slowly bring the pitch up until it sounds correct.

Singing

Singing along can also help. First listen closely to the reference pitch and sing it. Then sing the pitch the string is making. Usually, you will 'feel' whether you are singing higher or lower, and you can adjust the string accordingly.

In the middle

If you start with the fine tuners in their middle settings, you can typically tune each string up or down a whole tone or even more. In most cases, this is enough to get them to the correct pitches.

The D

Once the A is in tune, move on to the D-string. On the piano keyboard on page 11 you can see that this D is five white keys lower than the A. This musical distance, or *interval*, is called a *perfect fifth*.

Twinkle Twinkle

In case you don't have a piano to hand, you'll hear a perfect fifth when you sing the first two words of *Twinkle Twinkle Little Star*. To tune the D-string to the A-string, adjust it until the D followed by the A correctly produces the first two notes of the nursery rhyme.

Backwards

On the cello, all adjacent strings are a perfect fifth apart. As you usually tune from high to low (A, D, G, C), it may help to learn to sing *Twinkle, Twinkle* backwards: sing the second *Twinkle* while playing the higher-sounding string, and match the lower-sounding string to the first, lower-sounding *Twinkle*.

Check

When you've tuned all four strings, you need to check them,

and usually you'll have make a couple of small adjustments. At this stage forget *Twinkle Twinkle* – there's a better way to hear whether the instrument is perfectly in tune.

Two strings

The trick is to bow two adjacent strings. On a properly tuned cello, each pair of strings will produce a pleasant, full sound. If the sound seems slightly wavy, the strings are not quite in tune, so carefully adjust one of them. The slower the waves get, the closer you are – and when the waves disappear, you're in tune.

Press the string

If you still can't tell if a string sounds flat or sharp, try pressing it very close to the nut to raise the pitch very slightly. If this makes the pitch difference smaller (the waves become slower), you have to bring the string's pitch up a little.

Harmonics

The pitch difference between two strings becomes even clearer if you use harmonics. If you lightly touch the A-

Comparing string pitches with harmonics

a' on the D-string

a' on the A-string

string exactly midway, and the D-string at one third of its length, you'll find that they both sound a harmonic at the pitch a'. If not, you have to adjust one or both strings.

The other strings
This trick works for the other adjacent string pairs, too, of course: play the harmonic at one third of the lower-sounding string and compare it to the one midway on the next string up. You can easily play these two harmonics simultaneously, using your forefinger on one string and your thumb on the other.

Too much noise
A useful trick that allows you to hear the pitches of your strings very well, even on stage when everybody else is tuning up, is simply to press one of the two tuning keys of the bass strings to your ear. Try it.

Left or right?
Some cellists operate their fine tuners with their right hand, but others prefer to do it with their left. Though using your left hand requires you to reach around the cello, it means you can bow while you tune, which makes comparing pitches easier. A tip: whichever hand you use, be careful not to inadvertently press the fine tuners down while operating them. This will cause the pitch to drop as soon as you let go.

Bowing
When you're tuning, try to make sure you bow with a consist, light pressure. If you don't, the tuning may turn out to be less than perfect as soon as you start playing.

With a piano
You can, of course, tune all your strings to the relevant keys of a piano, but you'll learn to tune much better if you use the reference A only. After all, this is how you'll have to do it if you play in an orchestra or ensemble.

Press the pedal
If you do tune to a piano, the right pedal can be helpful. It allows the notes to sound for a long time, so you can leave the piano note ringing while you tune the cello to it.

Pitch pipes

Pitch pipes are little pipes that you blow into to create a note to tune to. There are two types: those with just one note (the A) and those with four (one for each string). Pitch pipes are very inexpensive, but they often don't last very long and sometimes their tuning can slip.

Electronic tuner

Another tuning aid is the electronic tuner, a device that 'hears' the note you are playing and indicates whether it is sharp, flat or just right. These devices, which range in price from around £5 to £50, are very popular with guitarists. However, cellists often say it's better to learn to tune by ear, because you depend on your ear to tell you whether you are playing in tune every time you stop a string.

Stretching strings

Strings stretch as they get older, and eventually they may get to a point where your fine tuners can't get them in tune any more. If so, you'll have to tune them a little higher with your pegs. Before you do, first loosen the string with the fine tuner as far as it will go. A tip: if a string has been stretched this far, the chances are that it needs to be replaced.

Tuning with pegs

When using the pegs to tune, it's also easiest to tune up rather than down. So if a string sounds sharp, first turn the peg until it's noticeably flat and then go up from there, turning the peg in very, very small increments. Apart from that, tuning with pegs is really the same as tuning with fine tuners, though it does take a bit of practice to get used to them.

Stuck pegs

Tuning with pegs from time to time, even if you use steel strings, has the added benefit that it will help prevent the pegs from getting stuck when humidity is high (in the summer) and from suddenly slipping and causing damage to the strings when the air is dry (in winter).

A=440

The A that most orchestras and ensembles tune to (a'), vibrates 440 times per second. This pitch is often referred to as A=440 hertz. A well-tuned cello A-string vibrates exactly half as fast (220 hertz).

Other tunings
Some orchestras tune to an A that is a tiny bit higher, such as A=442. For this reason, you can buy tuning forks in various different version of A.

Scordatura
For some works, most commonly in modern compositions, cellos are required to be tuned to different notes than the normal C-G-D-A. Such alternative tunings, which are known as *scordatura*, are usually employed to make certain chords easier to play. Three examples (from low to high) are D-A-D-A, B-F♯-D-A and C-F-D-A.

Detuning?
A final tip: do not reduce the tension of your strings after playing. This is more likely to hurt your instrument and strings than protect them.

10. CELLO MAINTENANCE

Cello repairs and adjustments are best left to an expert. But there are plenty of things you can do yourself to keep your instrument in the best possible condition: cleaning, replacing strings, straightening the bridge, finding buzzes, and more.

Rosin from your bow lands on your cello as dust. You can easily wipe most of it off with a soft lint-free cloth each time you finish playing. A cotton cloth such as an old, unprinted T-shirt or dishcloth will do fine. Don't forget to do the bowstick while you're at it. On some synthetic finishes you can use a slightly damp cloth if necessary.

Fingerboard and strings

It's best to use a different cloth for the neck, strings and fingerboard, which you touch with your fingers as you play. Wipe the strings with the cloth and then pull it between the fingerboard and the strings. Again, a cotton cloth is good for the job, but some cellists prefer to use silk.

Clean hands

Strings will live longer if you wash your hands before playing, and your cello will be easier to keep clean if you only hold it by the neck.

String-instrument cleaners

Every cello needs some extra attention once in a while, even if regularly wiped down. The top can get sticky and dull – especially between the *f*-holes, where most of the rosin ends up – and when this happens it's good to use some special string-instrument cleaner. Some of these products just clean, but there are also cleaners and cloths that polish your cello as well, smoothing away fine scratches.

Different varnishes

Which cleaner is most suitable for your cello may depend on its varnish, so always ask what you can and cannot use on an instrument when you buy or rent it.

Household products

Whatever you do, never use ordinary household cleaners on a cello, as you may seriously damage the finish. One exception is using a window cleaner on a synthetic or alloy tailpiece – as long as you spray the cleaner on a clean cloth first, rather than directly onto the instrument.

The fingerboard

You can occasionally give the fingerboard an extra clean by dabbing it with a soft cloth moistened with a tiny bit of rubbing (or denatured) alcohol. To make absolutely sure that no liquid gets onto the varnish of the body, keep the bottle well out of the way and do not allow the cloth to drag over it. To be extra safe, lay another (dry) cloth over the body before you start.

The strings

To remove rosin residue, grime and finger oils from your strings, rub them down with a clean cloth a few times, going from the top of the fingerboard to the bridge. Don't push too hard, though, and hold one hand across the strings, because they can really screech when you do this.

Alcohol and steel wool

If a clean cloth doesn't do the trick, you may want to moisten the cloth with a little rubbing alcohol, provided you're not using gut strings. Again, be very careful not to spill any of this liquid on the body of the cello. Special string cleaners are also available, and some repairers remove rosin build-up with very fine steel wool.

Inside

Over the years, dust and dirt will inevitably find their way inside your cello. Some players clean inside their instruments by pouring a handful of dry, uncooked rice through the *f*-holes and gently shaking the body around a few times. Then they turn the instrument upside down and keep shaking, which cleans the underside of the top and tips the rice, and most of the dust, back through the *f*-holes. If you use this technique, though, there's always a risk that a grain will get caught inside (in a tiny gap between the lining and the side, for example) and cause rattling, especially in instruments that are made roughly or have been frequently repaired.

Splinters
When cleaning your cello, make a habit of checking for splinters and other minor damage first, especially around the edges. If you find any, it's worth having them seen to – splinters can easily get caught on clothes or cleaning cloths and come off completely, and they can be quite dangerous too.

Professional cleaning
You need to take your cello to a professional repairer when it needs more serious cleaning: if there are stains that won't go away, if you can't get the neck clean, or if the varnish has become very dull (most commonly a problem under the strings or where you touch the body with your left hand). Many cellists have their instrument checked once a year, even if nothing seems to be wrong with it, just to be on the safe side.

Plastic
If your perspiration is very acidic, it may damage the varnish of your cello, and even the wood of the ribs where your left hand touches them. A solution employed by some repairers is to simply stick a strip of self-adhesive plastic to the rib. Some players and repairers are appalled at the very idea, but others see it as being perfectly practical.

TUNING PEGS AND FINE TUNERS
Fine tuners do not require much maintenance, if any at all. If one does get a little stiff, applying a tiny bit of acid-free Vaseline should do the trick. Wooden tuning pegs, on the other hand, can be troublesome.

Peg compound

The tuning pegs need to be able to turn smoothly, without slipping back. This usually requires the periodic use of a little *peg compound* or *peg dope*. Other cellists prefer tailor's chalk, also known as French or Venetian chalk. If these treatments aren't effective any more, you can clean the peg and peg hole with a little benzine. A stopgap solution for slipping pegs is to apply standard white chalk – but this will make the holes wear out faster. Some types of soap are also sometimes used, but soap can congeal and make tuning harder.

Loose

If a peg or its hole is badly worn, the peg may become very loose, in which case you may have to have a new set of bigger pegs custom-fitted to the instrument. The work will probably cost around £50–75, plus the same again for a good set of pegs (though much more expensive ones are available, with golden rings or other decorations). If the peg holes are really worn out, they can be rebushed.

BOW

Maintaining your bow is basically a matter of applying rosin to it, though very occasionally you should have the bow hair thoroughly cleaned or replaced.

Rosin

Applying rosin is only necessary when the bow hair gets too smooth, which shouldn't be more than once or twice a week, even if you play a lot. Move the bow hair over the rosin rather than the other way around, and apply the rosin along the full length of the hair, from the head to the frog. Keeping your thumb on the ferrule will prevent it from damaging the rosin.

Rosin tips

Avoid holding the rosin in the same position every time you apply it, as you may gradually wear a groove in it, leaving 'walls' of unusable rosin. Also, try not to touch the bow hair or the rosin with your fingers, as perspiration keeps the rosin from sticking to the hair. If you do need to touch the bow hair – to check the tension, for example – do so with the back of your hand. Finally, when using a brand-new cake of rosin, it may be necessary to scratch its surface with a pin to get it 'started'.

Excess rosin

After applying the rosin, wipe the bow hair with a cloth, or drag one of your nails across the hairs close to the frog. This makes sure that the excess rosin doesn't land on your instrument. You can shake out your bow instead, but it's best not to: even if you don't break anything or hit anybody, you may damage your bow. A tip: if your sound becomes coarse or uneven after applying rosin, you probably used too much of it.

Grimy near the frog

If the bow hair gets grimy near the frog, some players clean it with a cloth, slightly dampened with lukewarm water, possibly containing a touch of washing-up liquid. This is quite dangerous, though, as the little wooden wedges that hold the ends of the hair in place must be kept absolutely dry. If they get wet, they may expand and break the bowstick, thereby destroying the entire bow.

The bow hair is held in place by small wooden wedges

Cleaning the hair

If you need to apply rosin more and more often, it's probably due to old bow hair or a build-up of rosin residue. Again, some cellists clean the hair themselves, using a cloth very lightly moistened with rubbing alcohol – but it is much safer to have it done by an expert. The liquid can damage the stick, and you may end up with the hairs sticking together, rendering the bow unplayable. A bow maker or technician can also decide whether cleaning will help, or if rehairing is necessary.

Not tight

If you can't get the hair to the desired playing tension, it could be that your bowstick is losing its curve, in which case a bow maker or repairer may be able to restore it. However, it could be simply that bow hair has become overstretched. Sometimes the hair can be shortened, but often the best solution is a rehair.

Broken hairs

When hairs break, remove the loose ends by cutting them with the sharp edge of the ferrule or the face, rather than by pulling them out. Another solution is to cut them carefully with scissors, as close as possible to the ferrule or face. If too many hairs have broken, you'll need to take your bow for a rehair.

Rehair

Having your bow rehaired will probably cost you around £30–40. If you play for a few hours a week, the hair should last for years, and good-quality hair will not become wavy or brittle.

Frog and grip problems

If the frog doesn't slide smoothly any more and the screw button feels stiff, turn the screw button anticlockwise until it comes off and remove the frog, being very careful not to get the hair twisted. Cleaning the frog and the screw should do the trick, though you may need to lubricate the screw, in which case rub it on a candle – never use oil. If this doesn't work, take the bow to an expert. You'll also need to visit a professional if the frog wobbles or the bow grip needs to be replaced.

REPLACING STRINGS

If strings break or if their windings come loose, you'll need to replace them. The same is true if they're getting old, as older strings are more difficult to tune and sound duller. The better your cello, your playing and your ear, the sooner you'll notice when the strings need to be replaced.

A new set

If you replace one string, you may find that it sounds a lot brighter than the others. If so, the only solution is to replace the whole set. A tip: you may want to keep used strings, as they can come in handy as spares.

Leave two on
Never take off more than two strings at once, as you need at least two on the instrument at any time to keep the bridge and sound post in place. If the sound post does fall over, loosen all the strings and have it set in position by a repairer, who will have a special tool for the job.

Which order?
The two outer strings are more awkward to access in the pegbox, as the two middle strings get in the way. So, when changing your strings, remove a middle string first, then remove and replace the outer string next to it, and finally replace the middle string. For example, remove the D, remove the G, replace the G, replace the D. Then do the same with the other two strings.

Removing strings
When replacing strings, sit down and position the cello so that the scroll is on your left or right thigh. Take off the first string by slowly turning its tuning peg to release the string's tension. If the peg doesn't move, pull it out slightly. Then pull gently on the string, and the peg will start turning until the string comes loose. Guide the string between your thumb and index finger near the pegbox, so that it can't suddenly come loose and cause any damage.

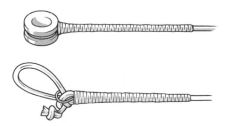

Most strings attach to the tailpiece with a steel 'ball', but gut strings often have a loop instead

Fitting strings
There are various different ways to fit a new string to a cello. One of the simple options is explained overleaf.

- Turn the peg so that the hole points diagonally upwards, facing the fingerboard.
- Hook the ball end of the string in the fine tuner or the tailpiece slot. If the string has a loop end, hook the loop in the tailpiece slot – don't feed the string through its own loop like a lasso unless the slot is worn out and won't hold the string.
- Stick the string through the peg hole (see illustration 1).
- Start winding it, turning the peg 'backwards' – in the direction of the scroll – whilst holding the string by the nut to stop it going slack and slipping out of the tailpiece (see illustration 2).
- Keep tightening the string, making sure that the windings run outwards, toward the thicker end of the peg. Use your index finger to keep the string tight and guide it through the groove in the nut (illustration 3).

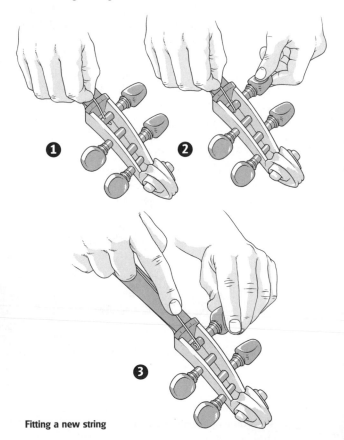

Fitting a new string

• Tune the string to roughly the right tension, using the strings that are still in place as a reference.

Kink

If a string keeps on coming loose from the peg as you try to tighten it, take a pair of pliers and make a kink about half an inch (1–1.5cm) from the end of the string. The kink will make the string hook itself in place as you begin to turn the peg.

Firmly fixed

If you want to be really sure that your strings will stay where they are, make a kink as described above, stick the string through the peg's hole and lay the kinked section flat against the peg. Then, as you turn the peg, let the string wrap around the kinked section a couple times. Never wind the plain unwound section of a string around itself in this way.

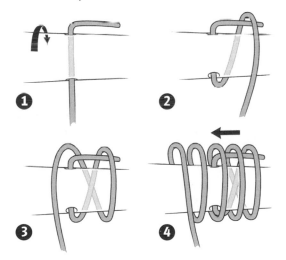

A good way to make sure the string doesn't slip

Too long

Sometimes you may find a that a string is a bit too long. If you have room in your pegbox, this shouldn't be too much of a problem: put the string through the hole in the peg, wind the string around the peg a couple of times, towards the edge of the pegbox, and then start winding the string back over the excess. Make sure, though, that the last few turns are wound directly onto the wood, not on top of the extra string. A tip: four or five windings should be enough to prevent a string from slipping. If you don't have the necessary room in your pegbox, you could cut the string, but, depending on the brand and series, this could damage it, so it may be worth thinking about trying a different type of string.

Space

Strings can break if they are jammed against the cheeks of the pegbox, so always make sure they have some space – unless you're in trouble because of a slipping peg (see page 97).

String sleeves

If you use string sleeves (see page 55), slide them into place when the strings are nearly tuned.

The first time

Replacing strings can be a bit tricky at first. You'll probably

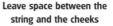
winding

cheek

Leave space between the string and the cheeks

wish you had two sets of hands when you're trying to simultaneously tighten a string, guide it through the groove in the nut and stop it from coming loose at the tailpiece. So its useful to have someone else around.

Peg problems

When you replace your strings, check the pegs at the same time. Grooves in the pegs can damage the strings, and if the holes are worn out the strings probably won't stay in place no matter what you do.

Sharp edges

Strings can also be easily damaged by sharp edges on the bridge, nut or peg holes, so check for these too, especially if one of your strings keeps breaking at the same point. Also make sure that the grooves in the nut are smooth and nicely rounded to prevent the strings from kinking. If a string doesn't run smoothly across the nut or bridge, try twisting the point of a soft lead pencil through the groove a few times – if that doesn't work, consult a professional.

Changing string type

If you intend to fit a set of strings of a different type to the ones you're currently using, there are a couple things to pay special attention to. First, if the new strings are thicker (for instance, if you replace steel strings with synthetic strings), the grooves in the nut and the bridge should be wide enough not to catch and damage the windings. Second, fitting higher or lower tension strings will raise or lower the string height. This can be compensated for by having the bridge adjusted, among other things.

Perfect fifths

If you have a good ear, here's another trick for testing the condition of your strings. On a properly tuned cello, there should always be a perfect fifth between one string and the next (see page 78). You can check this using a pencil to stop two adjacent strings in exactly the same position. Up and down the fingerboard, the difference in pitch should always be a perfect fifth, but if the strings need replacing this interval may vary a little, perhaps because one string is more stretched than the other. Bear in mind, though, that this could also be a problem with the alignment of the bridge. Also, if you use traditional gut strings you may not hear perfect fifths.

THE BRIDGE

A cello bridge has to withstand a lot of force, as the tension in the strings both pulls it forward and pushes it into the body. So it's worth keeping an eye on it.

Perpendicular

Now and then you should check that the bridge hasn't started leaning forward, toward the fingerboard. If it has, you may want to release the tension in the strings a little and carefully push the bridge back to its correct position, with the back perpendicular to the cello's top. If you'd rather, leave this to a violin maker or repairer.

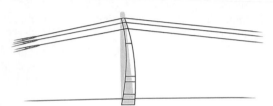

A bridge bending toward the fingerboard

In line

Also make sure that both feet of the bridge are lined up with the notches in the *f*-holes. If they're not, your instrument will probably not produce perfect fifths between the strings (see the previous page) and it will be hard to play in tune.

A new bridge

A bridge needs to be replaced if the downward pressure of the strings bends it or if the grooves have got too deep (no more than a third of the diameter of each string should be inside the groove). However, some repairers may restore the bridge rather than replace it, which will save you some money.

Other reasons

Another reason to have your bridge altered or replaced is that it's too flat, so that you accidentally play two strings instead of one, or too curved, which makes it difficult to play two or three strings at once. You may also need to replace your bridge if you change to a different type of strings.

Summer and winter bridges

You may well find that the string height of your cello changes throughout the year, as dry winter air makes the wood of cellos shrink. To compensate for this, some players keep two bridges: a higher one for use in the winter, and a slightly lower one for the summer months.

Custom-fitted

A new bridge needs to be custom-fitted to a cello, so that it has the right height and curve for the instrument and to make sure its feet match the top perfectly. Having a new bridge installed by a professional violin maker will generally cost around £50–75, the bridge itself being the least expensive factor. A new bridge should last for years.

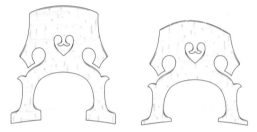

A blank bridge and one made to fit the instrument

More than just carving

You can get bridges with moveable feet that automatically adjust to the arch of the top. But even if you choose such a bridge, it can't hurt to have a specialist install it: again, fitting a bridge properly involves more than carving the feet.

OTHER PROBLEMS

A cello is a fragile instrument that only gives its best if everything is in place, nothing is loose that can produce a buzz, and nothing is worn out.

The sound post

If you have bought a new cello, it's a good idea to have it checked after six months or a year. One example of what an expert might spot is that the sound post may have become slightly too short as a result of the wood not having settled completely by the time you bought the instrument.

The tailpiece loop

Something else a repairer might notice is if the tailpiece loop has stretched. If it has, the distance between tailpiece and bridge will be too short, which may muffle the sound. On a full-size cello, the correct distance is about 4.5–5" (11.5–12.5cm), about one sixth of the instrument's string length. Tailpiece loops are often adjustable, so this can be set quite easily.

The fingerboard

Fingerboards eventually develop grooves from where the strings are stopped and very shallow pits from your fingers, especially if you perspire a lot when playing. Replacing a fingerboard is very expensive, because a lot of labour is involved, so the usual solution is to have the fingerboard reworked. Especially if you have a good ebony fingerboard, this isn't something you'll need to do very often – professional cellists who play for hours every day often have their fingerboards reworked every one or two years.

Loose pieces

If a piece of your cello breaks off, along the edge for instance, make sure that no moisture reaches that spot, and don't clean it. Take the instrument to a repairer as soon as possible and take the broken-off piece with you if you still have it. It's also best to see an expert if you find loose glue joints, or cracks. Don't be tempted to do any gluing yourself.

Buzzes

A cello can start buzzing for all sorts of reasons. Here are some examples:

- If the **bridge** or **nut** is too low the strings may vibrate against the fingerboard.
- The **winding** of a string may be damaged.
- **String ends** can vibrate if they are touching the pegbox or tailpiece.
- There could be something loose on one of the **fine tuners**.
- A loose **glue joint** may be the problem.

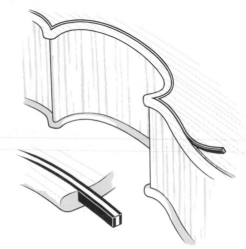

Purfling can work loose and cause buzzing

• **Wire mutes**, loose **purfling** and **decorative eyes and buttons** on tuning pegs can all cause unwanted noise.

HUMIDITY

Cellos, like many other wooden instruments, are very sensitive to dry air and to rapid changes in humidity or temperature.

Freezing

Dry air is especially likely to be a problem if it's freezing outside and the central heating is on full blast inside. If the humidity gets too low, the wood of your instrument will shrink. If you're lucky, the result will be that the string height is reduced a little and that you'll need a winter bridge (see page 94). If you're less lucky, the tuning pegs may suddenly come loose, which can result in string breakage, and it may get even worse – the top, back or any other parts can crack. The faster the humidity changes, the more dangerous it is.

Hygrometers

The best level of humidity, both for cellos and people, is generally said to be around fifty to sixty percent. A hygrometer is a device that allows you to keep an eye on humidity levels. Some expensive cello cases have one built in, but you may want to buy one separately to leave in the room where you keep your cello.

Humidifiers

If a hygrometer shows that the air is getting too dry or moist, it's time to do something about it. There are all kinds of small humidifiers that can be used inside a cello case, ranging from simple perforated rubber tubes with sponges inside to more complicated devices. Dampit is the best known trade name. Prices are usually between £3 and £15, and some models include a very basic humidity indicator. Cases with a built-in hygrometer often feature a humidifier as well.

Sluggish

A dial-type hygrometer, which uses a hair to measure the humidity level, may become sluggish and less responsive after about a year. To solve this, leave it outside for a night, and the moist air should refresh it for a whole year. When the weather gets colder and you switch the heating back on, you may also want to wrap it in a wet cloth for a quarter of an hour and then immediately set the pointer to 98%.

All-round solutions

If humidity is very low in your house, your cello, any wooden furniture or floors, and the people in the house may all benefit from a central humidifier (if the heating system allows it) or a portable one. Some examples of the latter are steam humidifiers (affordable, fast-working, but often noisy) and 'cold' humidifiers, which are quieter but more expensive, slower to work, and may need frequent maintenance (cleaning, filling, etc). Dehumidifiers are also available, to tackle very high humidity.

Some time to adjust

Always give your instrument some time to adjust to changes in temperature and humidity. For example, if it's freezing cold outside and you enter a warm room, leave your instrument in its case for fifteen minutes, or as long as you can. The more gradually things change, the less problematic it will be for your instrument. Another tip: always put your cello back in its case or bag as soon as you stop playing.

Heaters and vents

Even if your cello is in its case, be careful not to leave it in direct sunlight, near heaters, fireplaces or air-conditioning vents, or anywhere else where it may get too hot, cold, dry or wet.

ON THE ROAD

Here are a few tips for when you take your cello out and about:

- Make sure you have **a good case or bag**, and check now and again to make sure that the handles and carrying straps are properly secured.
- In a **car**, a cello is safest on the back seat. The temperature is likely to be better there than in the boot, and the

chance of damage if you have an accident is smaller too. But make sure the sun isn't shining directly on the bag or case.

- When **flying** with your cello, see if you can carry your instrument as hand luggage. If not, be sure to check it on as a fragile item.
- If you lose your cello, you're more likely to get it back if your **name**, **address and phone number** are listed inside the case or bag.
- Just to be on the safe side, always have a set of **spare strings** with you.

Insurance

Consider insuring your cello. Depending on their value, musical instruments usually fall into the category of 'valuables' for home insurance. This means you may have to let your insurance company know you have an instrument in order for it to be covered. And you may find that it can only be covered up to a certain value. Some home insurance policies also allow you to take out extra cover for your instrument, to protect it when you take it out of the house. This can be expensive, but it means your cello will be covered against theft and damage, whether you're on the road, at a rehearsal or on stage. You may also want to look into special musicians' insurance policies, which you'll often see advertised in string players' magazines. Whichever kind of policy you go for, always check the details carefully – some don't cover fractures caused by changes in climate, for example, and others have poor or no cover for air travel.

11. BACK IN TIME

This chapter provides a brief account of the cello's history, from the ancient *rebab* to the instrument we know today. Many books cover the subject in more depth, though if you read more don't be surprised to find lots of contradictory views: nobody knows exactly when the first cello was made and what happened at every stage since then.

Stringed instruments have been around since prehistory, probably growing out of the bow and arrow. Over time multi-stringed instruments developed, such as the ancient Greek lyre played in myth by Orpheus.

Bowing

Only much later was it discovered that you can make a string vibrate by bowing instead of plucking. Bowed instruments were probably being played in ancient Persia as early as the eighth century, and they were brought from Arabia to Spain not much later. One of these instruments was called the *rebab* or *rebec*.

Viols and violins

It is thought that the rebab was the predecessor of the two groups of instruments that later emerged in Europe: the *viola da gamba* family, also called *viols*, and the *viola da braccio* family, which included early violins and violas.

Arms and legs

Braccio instruments were played like the violin – 'on the arm', as the Italian word *braccio* indicates. But the viola da

Viola da gamba, a bowed instrument with frets and six strings

gamba family were played with the neck in an upright position, with their bodies rested on, or placed in-between, the musician's legs – *gamba* is Italian for 'leg'.

The cello

Because the cello is held between the player's legs, people often think it stems from the viola da gamba, but this isn't true. Viola da gambas are very different: they have sloping shoulders, a flat back, C-shaped soundholes, more strings and they are tuned differently. They also have frets – small ridges on the fingerboard that make playing in tune easier – as found on guitars.

Violone

In fact, the cello is based on the violin. When Flemish composers started to use lower-sounding voices in their works, some time in the fifteenth century, musicians needed lower-sounding instruments than the violins and violas of the day. Consequently, various larger versions of the violin were built. These instruments were known as *bass violins* or *violones*, the latter being Italian for 'large violin'.

Small large violin

The instrument that eventually became the cello was not the largest of these instruments, so the Italians called it *violoncello*, which literally means 'small large violin'. Much later, around 1765, violoncello started to be abbreviated to 'cello'.

Ferrari and Amati

When talking about the very first cellos, people often refer to the instrument shown on a fresco from 1535 by the Italian painter Ferrari. But the first known person actually to make cellos was the sixteenth-century violin maker Andrea Amati. His instruments, some of which have survived, are quite large, with bodies of about 31.5" (80cm). These larger cellos are often referred to as *church basses*.

Antonius Stradivarius

The development of the slightly smaller modern cello started in the late seventeenth century. Musicians wanted smaller instruments because they are easier to play: the string tension is lower and the distances between the positions on the fingerboard are reduced. Around 1707, Stradivarius, the most famous of all violin makers, started producing these smaller cellos, creating a standard model that's still being used today.

Violins versus viols

For a long time the violin family was looked down upon by the upper classes. They were used for dance music, in parades and so on, but 'serious' music was played on the more delicate and softer-sounding viols. However, the cello and the other members of the violin family eventually established total prominence over their rivals, and today viols are only commonly used for playing music from the period in which they flourished.

Solo

The violin was used as a solo instrument long before the cello: for many years, the cellist's role was restricted to accompanying other instruments, which is one reason why it was called bass or bass violin for so long. The first surviving compositions for unaccompanied cello date back to the late seventeenth century. Antonio Vivaldi (1678–1741) was one of the first composers to write solo concertos for the instrument.

End pin

The end pin was probably introduced in the 1840s by the Belgian cellist Adrian Servais, and was universally adopted in the second half of the century. Before this time, cellos were gripped between the player's calves.

The bow

The very first bows had an outward curve, like the type

you shoot arrows with, but this was gradually superseded by an inward-curve design. Around 1790, François Tourte (see page 64) designed the standard for today's bow.

From gut to synthetic
Wound strings were already in use in the mid-seventeenth century. Steel strings became popular in the 1920s, followed by synthetic-core strings in the 1950s.

12. THE FAMILY

The violin and viola are the cello's closest relatives, followed by the double bass. But it's also related to the hundreds of other bowed instruments that exist in the world, from the kemenche to the Hardanger fiddle. The cello's most modern relative, the electric cello, is covered at the end of this chapter.

As was explained in the previous chapter, the cello developed from the violin. It's not just a bigger violin, though. If you applied the violin's dimensions to the cello, its body would be about 40" (1m) long yet only around 3.5" (9cm) deep. Such instruments, sometimes referred to as *tenor violins*, have been built but they've never been popular.

The viola

The viola is just a bit larger than the violin. Its tone is not only slightly lower, but also a bit darker and slightly more nasal. A viola is tuned to the same notes as a cello, but an octave higher: the A-string sounds the same pitch as the standard tuning A (see page 11).

The double bass

The double bass, the lowest-sounding bowed instrument, looks like a mixture of the cello and the viola da gamba. It has the *f*-shaped toneholes and the fretless fingerboard of the cello and violin, but it usually has sloping shoulders like the viol family. A bass is tuned differently, too, the strings being a fourth apart, rather than a fifth. Like on a bass guitar, they're tuned to E-A-D-G, from low to high. Another difference is that a double bass has metal tuning

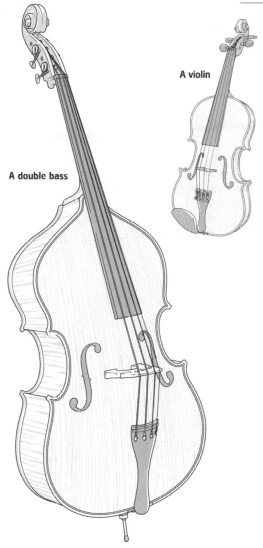

A violin

A double bass

machines, rather than wooden tuning pegs. The double bass is often used outside of classical music, especially in jazz, in which case it's plucked instead of bowed.

ETHNIC AND TRADITIONAL INSTRUMENTS

Most of the other members of the bowed string family are non-classical, and you'll usually find them only in the hands of musicians who play traditional music of certain regions.

Bourdon strings

The *viola d'amore* is one of the bowed instruments that has a set of regular strings as well as some *bourdon strings*, also called *sympathy strings* or *drones*. These strings are not bowed or plucked, but they vibrate 'sympathetically' when you play. The *lira da braccio*, an early version of the violin, also had bourdon strings.

Fele and rabab

Other bowed instruments with bourdon strings include the Norwegian *Hardanger fiddle* or *Hardangerfele* – a small violin that has four of them – and Afghan *rabab*, shown below, which has no fewer than twelve bourdon strings.

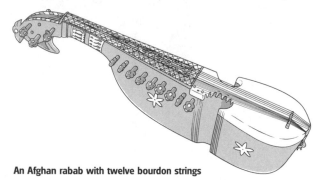

An Afghan rabab with twelve bourdon strings

Many names, many shapes

As discussed in the previous chapter, the predecessor of the violin was also called *rebab*. Today, this name is used for a wide variety of bowed instruments, some with and some without bourdon strings.

Kemenche, kamaché, kemângeh

The same goes for the *kemenche*. This name may refer to a small, pear-shaped instrument with three strings used in Turkish classical music. But it also describes an elongated three-stringed instrument used in folk music around the Black Sea and in Greece. The spelling varies as much as the shape, from *kemânje* to *kamaché* to *kemângeh*, and similar instruments are also sometimes referred to as rebabs (or rababs, *râbabs* and other spellings). They're usually played with their tail on the knee of the musician, with the neck held upright. Incidentally, you may even see musicians who play a regular violin that way.

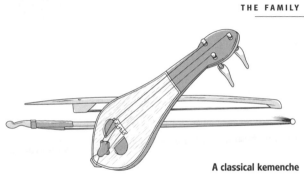

A classical kemenche

Fingernails

With some of these instruments, the different pitches are made not by stopping the strings on the fingerboard, but by touching them very lightly with a fingernail. Also, the bowstick is often straight, and you tighten the bow hair not with a frog but simply by putting your fingers or thumb between the stick and the hair.

Many more

Many other cultures have their own bowed-string instruments, from one-stringed examples in India to tubular Native American instruments. A complete list is beyond the scope of this book, but books dedicated to the subject are available.

CELLO VARIATIONS

As well as the tenor violin mentioned on page 104, many variations on the cello have been designed over the ages. Most of them disappeared within a decade or so of being invented, but some lasted a little longer.

Piccolo and tenor

The *violoncello piccolo* was a smaller cello with either four or five strings, and the *violoncello tenor* is one of the names used for instruments sounding an octave lower than the violin (in the same way that a cello sounds an octave lower than the viola).

Portable cellos

Other cello variations were developed to improve the instrument's portability. One example, the *violoncello portatile*, had a detachable neck that could be stored inside the rectangular body of the instrument. The *porta cello*, built around the middle of the twentieth century, featured a smaller but traditionally shaped body and retractable knee rests.

Indian music
Making variations on the cello is not just a thing of the past, but today's models are usually one-of-a-kind, custom-built instruments. One of the numerous examples is a five-string cello (D–A–D–A–D) with ten bourdon strings, designed to play Indian music.

ELECTRIC CELLOS
If you play your cello in a band, you're likely to find that it isn't loud enough. This can be solved by using either a regular microphone or a special pickup, but there are also special electric cellos designed specifically for playing amplified.

Electro-acoustic
You can amplify your instrument by fitting it with one or two *pickups* or *transducers*. These small, flat devices are usually wedged between the wings of your bridge. They literally 'pick up' the vibrations of the strings, and convert them to electric signals that can be amplified. An instrument with pickups can still be played unamplified (acoustically), so is sometimes described as an *electro-acoustic cello*.

Clip-on microphones
Some types of transducers (such as *piezo pickups*) can make your instrument sound less warm and natural than a microphone would. That's why some cellists prefer to use a miniature clip-on microphone. However, using a microphone can easily cause feedback (the loud shriek you hear when someone points a microphone at a loud-speaker), especially if you need to play loudly. A best-of-both-worlds solution is to use a pickup as well as a vocal microphone on a stand, and there are also systems that combine a pickup, a clip-on microphone and controls to set the balance between the two.

Electric cellos
If you only plan to play amplified, you could consider buying an electric cello. Instead of a soundbox, these

instruments have a small, often solid, body. Played without an amp, they make hardly any noise, which can be useful for practising purposes. Indeed, some electric cellos are specifically designed for that purpose (see page 17).

Chest and knee rests
So that you can hold them like regular cellos, small-bodied electric versions usually come with chest and knee rests. These are generally detachable for ease of transportation and storage.

MIDI
Some electric cellos also feature MIDI, allowing you to hook up your cello to synthesizers, effects devices, computers and other digital equipment. MIDI stands for *musical instrument digital interface.*

Shapes, designs and prices
Electric cellos come in a wide variety of shapes and designs, often with more than four strings and with tuning machines rather than the traditional wooden pegs. Some brand names in this field are Jensen Instruments, New Epoch, NS Design, Starfish Designs, Strauss, T.F. Barret, Violectra, and Zeta. Prices range from around £750 to about £7500.

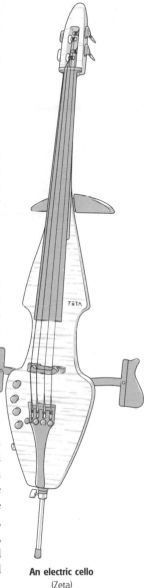

An electric cello
(Zeta)

13. HOW THEY'RE MADE

Good cellos are still made in much the same way as they were hundreds of years ago, with chisels, files, saws and planes. And it's no speedy process – making a cello top in the traditional way can take a master violin maker many days.

In a string instrument factory, machines are used for parts of the process, such as roughly shaping all the wooden components. However, some master violin makers still do everything by hand, from start to finish. In-between these two extremes are the workshops that buy cellos unvarnished, 'in the white', and finish them by hand and provide them with fittings and strings.

Quarter-sawn wood is stronger that slab-cut wood

Quarter-sawn

The top and back are usually made of *quarter-sawn* or *quartered* wood – wood that has been cut from the tree trunk in the shape of a slice of cake. Before each 'slice' is dried and seasoned it is sawn almost in half, which makes the wood less likely to warp, split or shrink later on.

Bookmatched

The slice is later sawed through completely to make two separate halves, which are folded open, like a book, and glued together. The result is the beginning of a *bookmatched plate*, with the two halves being mirror images of each other. Not all plates are bookmatched.

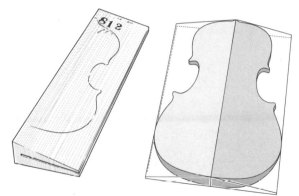

Folded open like a book, then glued together

Carved

Traditionally, the top and the back are then carved into shape. Using thickness gauges (*graduation callipers*) and touch, the violin maker keeps checking to see if any more wood needs to be removed. The exact thickness is important for the performance of the instrument.

Ribs, blocks and lining

The ribs of the instrument are either moistened or heated so they can be shaped, and then the top, bottom and corner blocks are glued on, which strengthens the joints. The rib structure is assembled around a wooden mould, and small strips of wood (the lining) are glued onto the ribs, so that the plates can be attached properly later.

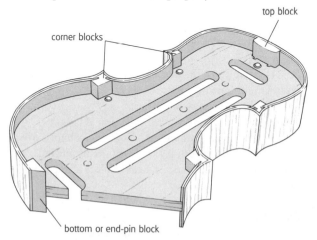

top block

corner blocks

bottom or end-pin block

The ribs are assembled around a mould

Cut from a single block ...

The neck

The neck, pegbox and scroll are carved from a single block of wood, which is then slotted into the top block. Before the heavy ebony fingerboard is added, it is made lighter by having its underside hollowed out.

Cut by hand

The *f*-holes and the channel for the purfling are traditionally cut by hand. This can take quite a long time, and so can making the bass bar, as it has to be made to fit the inside arch of the top exactly.

... and slotted into the top block

Mirror-smooth

The assembled cello is made mirror-smooth with a scraper, and is then finished with several coats of varnish. Violin makers often make their own varnish, so they can give it exactly the colour they want.

Bows

The bowstick is cut by hand and its curve is shaped over a flame. It is then varnished, fitted with its mountings, and finally the horsehair is added, held in place at each end by small wooden wedges.

The Italian masters

Many stories are told about what makes the great old cellos, violins and violas from Italy so special. It is sometimes said that the wood used to make them was soaked in seawater, and that the salt gave the instruments their special sound. Others say that the wood came from centuries-old church towers that burned down: the wood was first broken in by vibrations from church bells and then ripened by fire. Yet many experts claim that it's all in the varnish, which in those days sometimes contained all sorts of ingredients, including animal blood.

14. BRANDS AND MAKERS

When you go out to buy a cello, you'll come across dozens of makers' names – both real and imaginary – as well as the names of countless brands, countries, towns and regions. This chapter sheds some light on various aspects of the cello market, and introduces many of the popular brands and makers, including some famous old masters.

When you go shopping for a cello, you're bound to come across numerous German names. Germany has long had a great reputation for producing good instruments in every price range, and as a result many cellos bear a German name even though they were actually made in other European or Asian countries. Italian names are popular, too, because of the rich heritage of string-instrument making in that country.

Brand names

To add to the confusion, a single brand name may be given to cellos made by various different workshops or factories. And a single cello may have components from three different countries, be assembled in a fourth country, varnished in a fifth, and shop-adjusted by the distributor or dealer. So brand names on cellos do not often tell much about the instrument's origins.

Quality

On the other hand, of course, there are many companies that only put their label on good-quality carefully adjusted instruments, so their brand names can be seen as a guarantee for a certain quality. Some examples are **Becker**, **Otto**

Brückner, F. Cervini, Glaesel, Knilling, Meisel, Scherl & Roth, Wm. Lewis & Son and others mentioned below.

Germany
The German towns of Bubenreuth, Mittenwald, Klingenthal and Markneukirchen are famous for their violin-making traditions and for the instruments made there today. A few of the better-known names are **Götz**, **Höfner**, **Paesold** and **Stein**.

Eastern Europe
Many of the founders of German string-instrument companies came from the Czech city of Luby, which is often referred to as the 'Czech Mittenwald'. Other eastern European countries, such as Hungary, Romania and Bulgaria, also have long cello-making traditions, from low-priced factory-made student models to master instruments. Some names include **Dvorak**, **Lidl** and **Strunal** (Czech Republic), **Grygo Petrof** (Bulgaria), and **Bucharest** and **Vasile Gliga** (Romania). The Romanian centre of violin making is Reghin.

Asia
Cellos from China, Korea and other Asian countries have long had a poor reputation, and most Asian instruments are found in the lower price ranges. However, their quality is improving all the time – especially in the case of Chinese cellos – and German wood is sometimes used for the better models. Some examples of Chinese companies are **Ren Wei Shi**, **Samuel Shen** and **Xue Chang Sun**. **Nagoya Suzuki** is one of the better-known Japanese brands, mainly known for their fractional instruments.

France
France no longer produces large numbers of cellos, but two hundred years ago the French town of Mirecourt was home to the world's first string-instrument factory, employing some six hundred people. The prices of old French factory-made instruments are usually a little higher than those of comparable German cellos. It's often said that the French ones sound a little louder and brighter than the German models – but some claim to hear the opposite.

Other countries

In most countries you'll be able to find master violin makers who make high-quality instruments entirely by hand, usually to order. Most of them also sell used instruments, bows and accessories, and they repair and rebuild instruments, too.

Makers and masters

Not everybody who uses the name 'violin maker' is a master violin maker. Some mainly do repairs of student and intermediate cellos, for example, or concentrate on finishing and setting up white cellos (see page 110). It's impossible to say exactly how many master violin makers there are, but there are over a hundred in the US alone. Most countries have an association or federation of violin and bow makers, which you'll be able to trace on the Internet or in string players' magazines (see pages 124–126).

OLD MASTERS

The following paragraphs introduce some of the great names from the history of cello making. These are only the tip of the iceberg, of course, as quality instruments have been produced by thousands of people. There are books available that list hundreds of past makers, describing their instruments and listing typical current prices, but even books like these are very much incomplete, and quite likely not to list the maker of your own old cello.

Italy

The most famous Italian cellos were built in the town of Cremona, from the sixteenth century onwards by the likes of **Andrea Amati**, one of the very first violin makers. His grandson **Nicolò Amati** taught the craft to **Francesco Ruggieri** (also spelled as Ruggeri; 1620–c.1695), the most famous member of another important Cremonese violin-making family. Another of Nicolò's pupils was **Antonio Stradivari** (often referred to as Stradivarius), who lived from 1644 to 1737, and made harps and guitars as well as violins, violas and cellos. Around six hundred of his bowed instruments have survived. **Domenico Motagnana** (c.1680– 1750) and **Joseph Guarnerius del Gesu** (1698–

1744), the best-known member of the Guarnerius family, were among Stradivarius's students.

Outside Cremona
All of the makers listed above belonged to the Cremonese school, but there were also others. Each had its own characteristics, such as the shape of the *f*-holes or the precise shape of the body or scroll. Double purfling was one of the characteristics of the Brescian school, founded by Gasparo di Bertolotti, aka **Gasaparo da Salò**.

Germany
Jacob Stainer, who died in 1683, is often seen as the founder of German violin making. Until well into the eighteenth century, instruments made by Stainer were more expensive than those by Stradivarius, which were often considered 'too loud'. **Mathias Klotz I** (1656–1743), who was very important for violin making in Mittenwald, studied under Stainer and Nicolo Amati. Instruments made by his sons Sebastian and Georg are still highly prized.

Other countries
Two important French makers were **Nicolas Lupot** (1758–1824) and, from Mirecourt, **Jean-Baptiste Vuillaume** (1798–1875). The best-known English name is **Hill**, a company where various violin and bow makers worked. You often find the description 'Hill model' on tailpieces, tuning pegs, mutes and other parts. **Hendrik Jacobs** (1630–1704) and **Johannes Cuypers** (1766–1828) were two of the main Dutch violin makers, and the early American makers included **August Gemünder**, **Abraham Prescott** and **Benjamin Crehore.**

GLOSSARY AND INDEX

This glossary contains short definitions of all the cello-related words used in this book, and some others that you may come across in magazines and catalogues, or on the Internet. The numbers refer to the pages where the terms are used.

Adjuster See: *Fine tuners* and *Screw button.*

Antiquing *(27)* Technique to make cellos look older than they are.

Back, back plate See: *Top.*

Baroque cello *(34)* A mellow-sounding gut-stringed cello used for playing music of the Baroque era.

Bass bar *(9)* A wooden bar on the inside of the top.

Belly See: *Top.*

Body *(5, 29–31)* The body consists of the top, the back and the ribs (sides).

Bottom nut See: *Saddle.*

Bow *(9–10, 57–64, 86–88)* A stick strung with horsehair that is used to play the cello. A player's sound is heavily influenced by their bow. See also: *Bow hair, Frog* and *Stick.*

Bow grip *(10, 60)* A piece of leather or synthetic leather wrapped around the stick of the bow; also known as a *thumb grip.* Some people also use the term to refer to the silver, silk or imitation baleen winding or lapping next to the leather.

Bow hair *(58, 87–88)* The hair of a bow, which is either horsehair or synthetic.

Bridge *(6, 7, 34–37, 93–95)* The strings run over the

bridge, which passes their vibrations onto the top.

Button See: *End pin* and *Heel*.

Catgut The oldest material used for cello strings – sheep gut. The name comes from 'cattle gut'.

Cello in the white *(110)* An unfinished cello.

C-bout *(6)* The waist of the body.

Channel *(6, 8, 30–31)* The 'dip' near the edge of both the top and the back before the upward arching begins.

Cheeks *(6, 47)* The sides of the pegbox.

Children's cellos *(12–13, 56)* See: *Fractional sizes*.

Curl See: *Flamed wood*.

Double bass *(2–3, 104–105)* The lowest-sounding string instrument.

Ebony See: *Wood*.

Electric cello *(108–109)* An electric cello can be plugged straight into an amplifier, just like an electric guitar.

End pin *(6, 7–8, 41–43, 102)* The retractable rod – usually made of metal – on which a cello rests when being played. It is mounted in a plug, usually made of wood, called the *end button* or *end plug*. The end pin is also referred to as the *spike* or *rod*.

End screw See: *Screw button*.

Eye, Parisian eye *(38, 59)* Inlaid decoration found on tuning pegs, frogs and elsewhere. A Parisian eye is a mother-of-pearl dot with a small metal ring around it.

ƒ-holes *(5, 6, 112)* The two ƒ-shaped holes in the top of a cello.

Figured wood See: *Flamed wood*.

Fine tuners *(7, 39–40, 76, 85, 90, 96)* Small tuning mechanisms built into or attached to the tailpiece. Also referred to as *tuning*

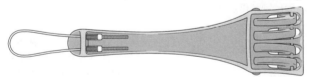

A tailpiece with an adjustable loop and built-in fine tuners

adjusters, string tuners and *string adjusters.*

Fingerboard *(5–6, 31–33, 95–96)* When you play you press down, or *stop*, the strings against the finger-board.

Fittings *(8)* The collective name for the cello's replaceable parts, including the tailpiece, pegs, nut and the fingerboard. Also known as the *trim.*

Flamed wood *(28)* Many cellos have a back and ribs that look as though they have been licked by flames. This flamed, *figured* or *curled wood* is usually more expensive than plain wood.

Fractional sizes *(12–13)* Cellos in small or *proportional* sizes, designed for children. Special fractional-sized strings are available for such instruments *(56).*

Frog *(58, 59)* One end of the hair on a bow is held in place inside the frog. At the bottom of the frog is the *slide.* Most frogs are *full-lined* with a metal *back plate.* At the front, where the hair enters the frog, it passes through the *ferrule* or *D-ring.*

F-stop See: *String length.*

Full-size cello *(12–13)* The regular 4/4-size cello. See also: *Fractional sizes.*

Fully carved *(111)* Fully carved instruments have tops and backs made by carving only.

Hair See: *Bow hair.*

Heel *(8)* The 'block' at the end of the neck, which strengthens the joint between the neck and the body. Also referred to as the *button.*

Insurance *(99).*

Lining *(111)* Thin strips of wood glued to the inside edges of the body.

Luthier Another name for a violin maker.

Maple See: *Wood.*

Master cello *(21–22)* A cello built by a master violin maker from start to finish.

Mensur ratio See: *String length.*

Mountings *(58)* The metal parts of a bow.

Mute *(16, 71–74)* A small device that can be attached to the bridge to make a cello sound a little sweeter and softer. *Practice mutes* muffle the sound a lot.

Neck *(6, 7, 31–34)* The wooden section that runs between the body and the pegbox. The fingerboard is attached to the neck.

Nickel silver *(58)* A mixture of copper, zinc and nickel. Also known as *alpaca*.

Nut *(6, 7, 32, 34)* The wooden strip over which the strings run at the top end of the neck. Also called the *top nut*.

Parisian eye See: *Eye, Parisian eye*.

Peg, pegbox *(5, 6)* The tuning pegs fit into the pegbox. See also: *Tuning peg.*

Peg compound, peg dope *(86)* Lubricant for tuning pegs.

Pegging The process of fitting tuning pegs to an instrument.

Pickup *(108)* A small and thin sensor that converts the vibrations of your strings into electrical signals, allowing you to plug your cello into an amplifier.

Plain wood See: *Flamed wood.*

Plates The back and the top of a cello.

Plug See: *End pin.*

Practice mute See: *Mute.*

Proportional instruments See: *Fractional sizes.*

Purfling *(6, 8, 28–29)* Inlaid decoration around the edges of the top and back, which also serves to protect the instrument from damage.

Quarter-cut, quarter-sawn wood *(110)* Wood cut from a tree trunk in segments (the way a cake is cut into slices). It is stronger and less likely to warp than *slab-cut* wood (for which the trunk is simply cut into planks), so is good for making thin yet sturdy tops and backs.

Ribbon See: *Bow hair.*

Ribs *(29)* The sides of the body.

Rod See: *End pin.*

Romberg *(32)* Romberg fingerboards have a flat area under the C-string.

Rosin *(10, 64–67, 86–87)* The sticky substance that is applied to a bow, allowing it to make the strings vibrate.

Saddle *(6, 7, 8)* A strip, usually of ebony, that prevents the top from being damaged by the loop that holds the tailpiece in place. Also known as *bottom nut.*

Screw button *(10, 59)* The component on a bow used for tightening and loosening the hair. Also called *end screw* or *adjuster.*

Scroll *(5, 6, 28, 112)* The scroll-shaped decoration at the top of the pegbox. Also known as the *volute* or the maker's *signature.*

Slide See: *Frog.*

Sound post *(9, 37–38)* Thin, round piece of wood wedged between the top and back. Sometimes referred to as the 'soul' of the cello.

Spike See: *End pin.*

Spruce See: *Wood.*

Stick *(10, 57–58)* The wooden (or sometimes synthetic) part of a bow.

Stop See: *String length.*

Stradivarius *(23, 24, 116)* Antonio Stradivari, often referred to as Stradivarius, is the world's most famous violin maker. He designed the standard cello model.

String adjusters See: *Fine tuners.*

String height *(34, 54, 94)* The distance from the strings to the fingerboard, measured at the end nearest the bridge.

String length *(12, 29)* Usually refers to the length of the strings between the nut and bridge, which is also called the *speaking length.* Violin makers also use the term *f-stop*, which describes the distance from the top edge of the body to the notches of the *f*-holes. The ratio between this distance and the distance from the top edge of the body to the nut is referred to as the *stop, neck to stop ratio* or *mensur ratio.* In cellos the ratio is usually 10:7, but differences do occur, even between cellos with identical string lengths. A tip: a different mensur ratio to the one you're used to can make you play out of tune at first.

String tuners See: *Fine tuners.*

Strings *(10–11, 49–59)*, **replacing strings** *(88–93)* Cello strings are available in gut, synthetic-core and steel-core versions, and with windings made of various different kinds of metals.

Table See: *Top.*

Tailgut See: *Tailpiece, tailpiece loop.*

Tailpiece, tailpiece loop *(6, 7, 40–41)* The strings are attached to the tailpiece, and the tailpiece is attached to the end button with the tailpiece loop or *tailgut.*

Top *(5, 6, 29–31)* The top of the body, which is one of the most important components of a cello. It's also known as the *table, belly* or *plate,* and the opposite side is called the *back.*

Top nut See: *Nut.*

Trim See: *Fittings.*

Tuning *(38–40, 76–82)* Cellos are tuned using tuning pegs or fine tuners.

Tuning adjusters See: *Fine tuners.*

Tuning pegs *(5, 6, 38–40, 76, 90–92)* Cellos are tuned using four tuning pegs, often in combination with one or more fine tuners.

The peg head is known as the *thumb piece.* See also: *Fine tuners.*

Varnish *(26–27, 113)* The type of varnish used on a cello is important for its sound and appearance. Different varnishes should be cleaned in different ways.

Viola, violin *(2–4, 100–102, 104, 105)* Two very close, much smaller relatives of the cello.

Volute See: *Scroll.*

White cello *(110)* An unvarnished cello.

Winding See: *Bow grip* and *Strings.*

Wolf note *(74–75)* An unwanted stuttering sound that affects many cellos. They can be reduced in many different ways.

Wood *(30, 31, 57)* Various different types of wood are used in cello production. Common examples are spruce (for the top), maple (for the back) and ebony (for the fingerboard).

WANT TO KNOW MORE?

This book gives you all the basics you need for buying, maintaining and using a cello. If you want to know more, try the magazines, books, Web sites and newsgroups listed below.

MAGAZINES AND NEWSLETTERS

The two magazines at the top of the following list offer lots of articles on cellos, violins and violas, covering makers, strings, repair, playing and more. The other entries are the newsletters or journals from string-instrument organizations, and tend to be mainly aimed at professionals.

- *The Strad* (UK) www.orphpl.com
- *Strings* (USA) www.stringsmagazine.com
- *Newsletter of the British Violin Making Association* (UK) www.bvma.org.uk
- *Journal of the Violin Society of America* (USA) www.vsa.to
- *American Lutherie* (USA) Focuses on stringed-instrument making and repair, including guitars and other fretted instruments. www.luth.org

BOOKS

There are dozens of books on the cello. The following is a selection of publications that cover some of the subjects of this book in greater depth.

- *Cello (Yehudi Menuhin Music Guides)* by William Pleeth (Kahn & Averill, 2001; 290 pages; ISBN 1 871 08238 2).
- *Cambridge Companion to the Cello* by Robin Stowell (editor) (Cambridge University Press, 2000; 269 pages; ISBN 0 521 62928 4).

- *Cello Story* by Dimitri Markevitch (Summy Brichards Inc, 1984; 182 pages; ISBN 0 874 87406 8).
- *The Cello* by Elizabeth Cowling (B.T. Batsford, 1975; 224 pages; ISBN 0 713 42879 1).
- *The Health of the Violin, Viola & Cello: Practical Advice on the Acquisition, Maintenance, Adjustment & Conservation of Bowed Instruments* by Lucien Greilsamer (Henry Strobel, Violin Maker and Publisher, 1991; ISBN 0 962 06734 2).

Making a cello

There are numerous written for amateur and professional violin makers, which also may be of interest if you just want to know more about the instrument. Some examples:
- *Cello Making, Step by Step* by Henry Strobel (Strobel, 1995; ISBN 0 962 06737 7). This book should be used with *Violin Making, Step by Step* by the same author (Strobel, 1994; ISBN 0 962 06736 9).
- *Violin Making: A Guide for the Amateur* by Bruce Ossman (Fox Chapel Pub, 1998; 96 pages; ISBN 1 565 23091 4).
- *Violin and Cello Building & Repairing*, by Robert Alton (Library Binding, 1990; 82 pages; ISBN 0 781 20517 4).

THE INTERNET

On the Internet there are countless sites for cellists, often with all kinds of articles, discussion groups, FAQs (Frequently Asked Questions) and links. The following are some good starting points:
- Internet Cello Society: www.cello.org
- Violink: www.violink.com
- Maestronet: www.maestronet.com
- Cello City (covers non-classical cellos and cello playing): www.newdirectionscello.com

Teachers and repairers

If you're looking for a teacher or a professional repairer, there are various organizations that may be able to help you. If you want to locate a violin maker in the UK, try contacting the British Violin Making Association (www.bvma.org.uk). And to find a teacher, you could try: the Incorporated Society of Musicians (www.ism.org), the European String Teachers Association (www.estaweb.org.uk) or the Federation of Music Services (http://fp.federationmusic. f9.co.uk).

Makers

The Internet is also a good place to seek out information about the maker of your own cello – try simply entering the maker's name into a search engine. If you are interested in the great old masters, take a look at The Smithsonian Institution site (www.si.edu/resource/faq/nmah/music.htm)

ESSENTIAL DATA

In the event of your instrument being stolen or lost, or if you just decide to sell it, it's useful to have all the relevant data at hand, either for yourself, your insurance company or for the police. You can jot down this information on these two pages. There's also room to list the strings you're currently using, for future reference.

INSURANCE

Company:	
Phone:	Fax:
Agent:	
Phone:	Fax:
Policy number:	
Insured amount:	
Premium:	

CELLO

You'll find some of the details of your cello on the label, which – if there is one – is usually visible through the ƒ-hole on the side of the C-string. Some cellos have labels that can only be read when the body is opened. The name of the maker can also be branded in the body, for example on the back, close to the heel.

Make and model:

Manufacturer/violin maker:

Serial number:

Colour:

Make of bridge:

Tailpiece   make:

              type:

              colour/material:

Description of tuning pegs:

Any repairs, damage or other distinguishing features:

Date of purchase: Price:

Place of purchase:

Phone: Fax:

BOW

Make/maker:

Type: Price:

Octagonal/round:

Mounting:

Date of purchase:

Place of purchase:

Phone: Fax:

STRINGS

It's worth making a note of the strings you put on your cello, so you can use the same ones again if you like them – or avoid them if you don't.

string	make	type	thickness/tension	date
1st: A				
2nd: D				
3rd: G				
4th: C				

string	make	type	thickness/tension	date
1st: A				
2nd: D				
3rd: G				
4th: C				

string	make	type	thickness/tension	date
1st: A				
2nd: D				
3rd: G				
4th: C				

ADDITIONAL NOTES

....
....
....
....
....
....
....
....
....
....
....
....
....
....
....
....